deep relief
NOW

simple keys for quickly healing
your longstanding emotional pain

Dennis and Dr. Jen Clark

For video demonstrations and further teaching:
www.forgive123.com
www.DeepReliefNow.com

Copyright © 2011 by Dennis and Dr. Jen Clark

Deep Relief NOW
Simple Keys for Quickly Healing Your Longstanding Emotional Pain
by Dennis and Dr. Jen Clark
www.DeepReliefNow.com

Printed in the United States of America

ISBN 9781619043190

Unless otherwise indicated, Bible quotations are taken from the New King James Version. Copyright © 1982 by Thomas Nelson, Inc. Used by permission.

Scripture quotations marked AMP are taken from the Amplified Bible. Copyright © 1954, 1958, 1962, 1964, 1965, 1987 by The Lockman Foundation. Used by permission.

Scripture quotations marked MSG are taken from The Message. Copyright © 1993, 1994, 1995, 1996, 2000, 2001, 2002 by NavPress. Used by permission.

Scripture quotations marked NLT are taken from the New Living Translation. Copyright © 1996 by Tyndale House Publishers, Inc. Used by permission.

Scripture quotations marked NIV are taken from the New International Version. Copyright © 1973, 1978, 1984, 2011 by Biblica, Inc. Used by permission of Zondervan.

Scripture quotations marked NASB are taken from the New American Standard Bible. Copyright © 1960, 1962, 1963, 1968, 1971, 1972, 1973, 1975, 1977, 1995 by the Lockman Foundation. Used by permission.

Scripture quotations marked PNT are taken from The Power New Testament. Copyright © 2003 by Shalom Ministries. Used by permission.

www.xulonpress.com

"DEEP RELIEF NOW has precious gems of "gut level" tools of release and restoration—it is a must-read for the turbulent times we are navigating through. This book is a brilliantly honest assessment of the what, why, and how-to's to deal with the burden of the unhealed. Get two copies and give one away!

—*Mickey Robinson, Prophetic Destiny International*

For over 30 years, Mickey Robinson has been in fulltime ministry sharing the reality of God's power to change people's lives. He is the author of *Falling Into Heaven*, the dramatic account of Mickey's near-death experience from the edge of eternity. He incurred catastrophic injuries in an airplane crash followed by miraculous healings and a spiritual adventure of a new life on earth. Mickey and his wife, Barbara, live in Franklin, Tennessee.

"DEEP RELIEF NOW is an essential primer on how to set yourself free from a multitude of hurts, experiences and relationships that have pursued you and prevented you from enjoying the Shalom that is available to you. Whether you are a brand-new convert or not even a convert yet—or you have been in ministry for years—the chances are very strong that there are things holding you back from fulfillment of your heavenly assignments. DRN is a book that will walk you through the steps to freedom, the shalom given to you in John 14:27. Translated "Peace," Shalom is much more than that: Shalom means that everything is complete, there is ample provision, no conflict, Divine Health, every relationship is in order; there is no injustice, no pain!

Deep Relief Now takes you through a process, and on the way you will enjoy the testimonies of Dennis and Jennifer. You will sense their personalities and develop a relationship, just by reading their stories. The style as they weave their ministry for you will hold your attention and hold your hand as you walk through the process. The focus on forgiveness is a major building block of Christian living, often a stumbling block which both Dennis and Jennifer help you to overcome.

My final thought about DRN is NTS—it is NONE TOO SOON for you to be digesting this material! Digesting it turns it into action, setting you free."

—*William J. Morford, Shalom Ministries,*
author/translator of *The Power New Testament,*
www.thepowernewtestment.com

Sid Roth, President of Messianic Vision, says of The Power New Testament, "A magnificent work! The only New Testament I've used since I got it." The Power New Testament is a fresh translation of the Fourth Edition United Bible Society Greek Text, bringing out power in the Greek language that is frequently overlooked. It also translates Hebrew idioms that are commonly missed and explains Jewish customs.

*I am leaving **peace** with you, I give My **peace** to you: I am giving to you, not just as the world would give. Your heart must not ever trouble you and it must stop being timid (John 14:27 PNT).*

"WHEN IT COMES TO LIFE TRANSFORMATION, the heart of the matter is always a matter of the heart. In this groundbreaking book, Dennis and Dr. Jen Clark provide a timely prescription for what ails the human heart. Though you may have already tried countless other remedies to relieve your emotional pain, don't give up— here's a simple, speedy approach that really works!"

—*Jim Buchan, Crosslink Ministries*

Jim Buchan has been a pastor, an attorney, and the editor of MinistriesToday Magazine and The MorningStar Journal. His articles have appeared in more than 40 publications worldwide. Jim is the author of several books, including *Apostolic Evangelism* and *Walking the Leadership Highway—Without Becoming Road Kill!*

CONTENTS

preface:
WHY YOU NEED THIS BOOK..................................7

part one • 11
DR. JEN'S STORY: a counselor in need of healing

chapter one
THE DAY THAT CHANGED EVERYTHING 13

chapter two
YES, EVEN COUNSELORS NEED DEEP RELIEF 17

part two • 23
DENNIS' STORY: a pastor at the end of his rope

chapter three
BEAUTY FOR ASHES. 25

chapter four
RENDEZVOUS WITH DESTINY 33

part three • 37
OUR STORIES INTERSECT: making all things new

chapter five
THE SOUND OF A VOICE 39

chapter six
FROM PRAYER PARTNERS TO LIFE PARTNERS.............47

part four • 53
DRN DISCOVERED

chapter seven
HITTING BOTTOM, FINDING FORGIVENESS.............55

part five • 67
THE POWER OF SIMPLE PRAYER

chapter eight
LOCATION, LOCATION, LOCATION **69**

chapter nine
LEARNING ANOTHER LANGUAGE **83**

chapter ten
LORD, TEACH ME TO PRAY! **95**

chapter eleven
LEARNING INTIMATE PRAYER **101**

part six • 109
HEALING PRAYER

chapter twelve
WHAT MUST I DO TO BE SAVED? **111**

chapter thirteen
CHRIST THE FORGIVER **125**

chapter fourteen
EASY DOES IT **133**

chapter fifteen
THE GOD TOOLS **153**

chapter sixteen
FORGIVE 123 . . . . **175**

chapter seventeen
ARE YOU READY TO RECEIVE DEEP RELIEF NOW? **185**

appendix:
TRUE STORIES OF LIVES IMPACTED BY DRN **189**
WHAT CHRISTIAN LEADERS ARE SAYING **202**

preface:
WHY YOU NEED THIS BOOK
——— A WORD FROM DENNIS ———

PEOPLE ARE HURTING. As a pastor, I see it every day.

But you don't have to be a pastor to see that people are hurting. The evidence is everywhere.

Tabloids at the grocery store describe in large fonts how celebrities are experiencing meltdowns in their marriages, children, careers, sobriety and even their sanity. They're rich and famous and seem to "have it all"…yet they are hurting.

But you don't have to be a celebrity to experience emotional pain. It happens to all of us. Fortunately, we don't have the paparazzi following us around with their cameras, but God sees our pain. And He wants to help. That's why Jen and I wrote this book.

This is not just another book on counseling or self-help. As you can see from the title, Jen and I are making a very bold and audacious claim. No matter how deep or longstanding your pain may be, if you follow the simple solutions this book offers, you can experience…

DEEP RELIEF NOW!

Perhaps you've lost hope in traditional counseling and therapy…and so have we! But in contrast to the largely ineffective methodology you may have tried in the past, we've discovered an approach that can provide *deep relief for your deepest hurts*!

Look at what this means…

- **Relief.** If you've received no lasting relief despite spending thousands of dollars on traditional forms of psychotherapy, you're not alone. Perhaps you feel like this woman described in the Bible: "A long succession of physicians had treated her…taking all her money and leaving her worse off than before" (Mark 5:26 MSG). The proven method presented in this book has brought true and lasting RELIEF to countless people—and it can provide relief to YOU as well!

- **Deep.** Many people don't believe it's possible to actually *heal* their deepest hurts. So what's the next-best thing? Medication! Instead of seeking deep relief, they settle for solutions that merely mask the symptoms. And let's be honest: Modern pharmaceuticals often *do* provide a measure of relief. Many people are able to carry out relatively normal lives by numbing their pain and elevating their mood through seemingly miraculous medications. But ask yourself this: Would you rather relieve your headaches through endlessly popping Advil, or would you rather eliminate the underlying conditions that are causing your headaches in the first place? This book is about good news: *You can experience deep and lasting relief of your underlying emotional hurts.*

- **NOW!** The message communicated by most of the professional counseling community today sounds a lot like some chiropractors I've met: "I can't really *heal* you, but if you come in for regular appointments over the course of many years, I can at least make your pain manageable." This model of therapy makes patients ever-more dependent on the therapist, never fully able to stand on their own. However, **Deep Relief NOW** means just what it says…

YOU CAN RECEIVE TRUE AND LASTING RELIEF…

RELIEF THAT IS DEEP RATHER THAN SUPERFICIAL.

AND YOU DON'T HAVE TO WAIT FOR YEARS OF COUNSELING—

YOU CAN EXPERIENCE THE RELIEF NOW!

Before we go on to share how this all works, Dr. Jen (my lovely wife) and I want to share our own story of experiencing this amazing discovery for ourselves.

A WORD FROM DR. JEN

Dennis and I wrote this book not just to tell you OUR story, but to pave the way for God to break into YOUR story. We want to give you something that works— something that will bring deep relief from the pain and frustration you're currently experiencing.

Why do we want you to share Deep Relief Now (DRN) with you? Because we know you don't have to remain in inner turmoil and distress.

You've probably already tried to address your pain in many different ways, so we understand if you're skeptical that DRN can help. But that's why I wanted to share my own story. Despite all my degrees, diplomas and research, my inner hurts remained. Yet the simple truths of DRN brought me internal freedom I never thought possible.

What God taught Dennis and me, you can learn too. If you follow the easy-to-grasp process, you can have the same result. After seeing thousands of lives touched, we are confident that no pain is too severe or too deep for the Lord to relieve, quickly and permanently.

Dennis learned DRN over the course of 35 years of experience as a pastor and counselor. Now we're able to put it into a simple format that works for anyone, at any age, and at any time.

You can take DRN as far as you want. Whether you just want to quickly deal with a few wounds or receive a total life transformation like me, these principles are powerful, life-changing tools. And it's our prayer that, as God uses DRN to change your own life, you will want to help others as well.

So what are you waiting for? Like Dennis and me, you can experience deep relief from your emotional pain—and you can experience it NOW!

—part one—

DR. JEN'S STORY:
a counselor in need of healing

chapter ONE
THE DAY THAT CHANGED EVERYTHING

———————————— BY DR. JEN ————————————

WE WERE TWO STRANGERS—a pastor named Dennis and me, a Christian psychologist—traveling from different parts of the country to attend a conference in Jacksonville, Florida. I had been to plenty of conferences before, but none changed my life like this one.

During one of the sessions, a young woman named Amanda suddenly had an emotional meltdown. Completely freaking out, she collapsed onto the floor, weeping uncontrollably.

Nobody helped. Here we were at a Christian conference, and nobody did anything to relieve her distress. Instead, everyone simply froze in their tracks, staring in shock as the tormented young woman writhed on the carpet.

As a psychologist, I *wanted* to help her, but what could I offer? As I quickly took inventory of the psychological tools in my toolkit, I thought to myself, "Five or 10 years of counseling *might* give her some relief!"

But what about NOW? Could anything be done to relieve Amanda's distress?

After a brief moment of hesitation, the pastor came over and calmly knelt beside the hysterical woman. Step by step, he began to coach her, and Amanda's intense emotional pain was quickly and easily transformed into deep peace.

It was an amazing scene! In less than 10 minutes, the distraught young woman was up on her feet, smiling and calm, testifying that her emotional pain was gone. Yes, it was GONE!

As a psychologist, this was a mind-blowing experience for me. I had all sorts of education, training and degrees in how to give people relief from their emotional pain, but I had never seen anything like this. While my approach was well-meaning and theoretically sound, I was struck that this pastor's approach *really worked*. It not only brought *deep relief*, it brought it *fast*.

Astounded, I exclaimed to myself, "This is HUGE!" In a flash, I saw what such rapid and thorough emotional healing could mean to a world full of hurting people.

My life has never been the same since that day when I saw a young woman's life transformed in mere moments. That's also the day I met Dennis—the pastor, who is now my husband—and he started teaching me about the revolutionary tool we call Deep Relief Now (DRN).

There Had to Be More

Before that pivotal day in Jacksonville, I had become very disillusioned in my role as a Christian counselor. With all my heart, I wanted to see people find real relief from their problems. Yet most of my clients and friends either made progress that was extremely slow—or they seemed to make no progress at all.

One medical doctor told me of his frustration in trying to help people in his church overcome various addictions, "I know the Bible says believers are supposed to be new creations in Christ, but I see the same old never-ending issues." Another counselor shared her conclusion that a person had to be pretty well-adjusted at the time of salvation, or else they were most likely too wounded to ever be of much use in Christian ministry.

Despite seeing these discouraging results, I clung to the hope that *somewhere* there must be solutions that actually brought people emotional healing. Like a relentless investigative reporter, I went on a personal quest to discover some key the counseling community had perhaps overlooked.

I studied. I prayed. I interviewed counselors who were considered "experts." From psychoanalysis to Christian inner healing and deliverance, I didn't want to leave any stone unturned in my pursuit. I investigated the role of medication, support groups, and altar calls—but still I felt like I was only scratching the surface in trying to solve people's deep-seated emotional and behavioral problems.

What About You?

Perhaps you've experienced this same frustration in trying to find relief for yourself or the people you love. You feel as though you've tried everything, yet the inner turmoil remains.

Before we go on to examine and experience DRN (Deep Relief Now), I encourage you to do an honest personal assessment of your need for emotional healing. Ask yourself questions like these:

- Have you ever felt out of control and unable to stop yourself from doing some kind of undesirable behavior?

- Do you struggle with unrelenting fear, emotional pain, or feelings of rejection or inferiority?

- Have you tried a variety of remedies—spiritual or secular, self-help or professional—with only limited relief?

- Have you reached the point where you are no longer expecting to get any better?

Perhaps you are one of *millions* of people in our country who have "sought help" from a professional counselor. If so, I applaud you for seeking solutions to your problems.

However, you need to be honest with yourself. As Dr. Phil likes to ask people, "How's that workin' for you?"

If you are like countless people...

- After years of counseling, psychotherapy or support groups, your pain remains.

- Medication has given you partial relief, but you suspect that it's just covering up the symptoms, not bringing you actual healing.

- The bottom line is that you've spent thousands of dollars on remedies that haven't really worked.

If you've experienced this frustration in your life or seen it in the lives of your loved ones, isn't it time for a change? In the next chapter, I pull back the curtain on my own struggles and share more about how God transformed Dennis and me through the discovery of Deep Relief Now.

chapter TWO
YES, EVEN COUNSELORS NEED DEEP RELIEF

by Dr. Jen

DID YOU KNOW THAT many people who become counselors don't have it all together in their own lives? If they say they do, then just ask their spouse or children if they are truly healed of all their issues.

Often people go into psychology or counseling in an attempt to find solutions for their own inner pain. Hopefully, their pain has also caused them to have compassion for others, but that doesn't mean their own struggles have been resolved. Usually they just learn to cope with life's challenges and maintain their outward composure in spite of their hidden emotional turmoil.

This is what my life as a psychologist was like when I attended the conference in Jacksonville. Most of the time I managed to present an appearance of professional confidence and decorum, but beneath the surface, I was experiencing hidden torment. Despite all my psychological training, I was still trapped in my past—bound by secret hurts, wounds, fears, anger and shame.

Yes, my training had given me lots of tools for emotional healing, but there was just one problem: The tools were largely ineffective! Instead of bringing me actual transformation and healing, these tools caused me to push my issues even deeper.

However, when God used Dennis to show me the amazing principles of Deep Relief Now, I didn't have to bury or "stuff" my issues anymore. In a remarkably short period of time, my internal conflict vanished. For the first time in years, I could…

- Be childlike without being childish

- Laugh without crying on the inside

- Express my heart without being demanding or controlling

- Deal with conflicts without flying into emotional outbursts

When I realized the awesome depth of my transformation, I felt like shouting at the top of my lungs, "Free at last! Free at last! Thank God Almighty, I'm free at last!"

How Did I *Get* These Hang-ups?

Those who meet me today often conclude that I've always had a pretty carefree life. So they're puzzled when I am describing my hidden inner turmoil before meeting Dennis and finding out about DRN.

Well, like you, I've discovered life isn't always easy. So let me tell you some more about my story …

Born and bred in Tallahassee, Florida, I was a head-strong child with a domineering father. We frequently butted heads, and I found myself angry at his control and angry at *myself* for not being assertive enough to get my way.

As a result of the personality clashes with my dad, I internalized a lot of resentment and pain. Feeling intimidated and fearful, I was well-behaved on the outside, but on the inside there was a little rebel.

Fortunately, I concentrated on my schoolwork and avoided getting in with the wrong crowd. My dad saw my good grades and strong work ethic, and he concluded my only acceptable career options were to become a doctor or an attorney.

Well, I decided I wanted to be a psychologist instead. My father considered this a *terrible* choice and told me, "That's no better than becoming a witch doctor!"

Marriage, Children…and Widowed

When I was just 21 years old, I married a physician named George and moved to the small town of Waycross, Georgia. Over the next few years, I had two children, did some mountain climbing, went to graduate school, and got saved.

Having Christ in my life was a great adventure, and I was thrilled by the changes He brought. However, George was running from God, and he was distressed by my decision. He thought I must have thrown my brains out the window in order to "believe all that Bible stuff."

Although persecution can strengthen your faith and build your character, it also can rip your heart to shreds when a person you love says harsh words to you and ridicules your relationship with the Lord. I found that the anger and fear of my childhood were compounded by a new level of pain and sorrow.

George's anger and rejection caused me to suffer greatly. But somehow the Lord showed me that this resentment was not really toward me, but toward Him.

The pain was unbearable at times. Even though I shed many tears, my psychology training helped me understand my "issues" and learn to cope with my situation. Years later, I would learn that Jesus wants us not just to *cope* with life, but to *enjoy* it: "I came that they may have and *enjoy life*" (John 10:10 AMP).

You see, until I learned it's possible to have *deep relief* from our hurtful feelings, coping was the best outcome my psychology studies could offer. Superficial relief, after all, was better than no relief at all.

New challenges arose in 1993, when my husband died of lymphoma. George had gone through a traumatic two-year battle, but the cancer eventually won. Thankfully, my pastor had driven to the hospital in Atlanta and led George to the Lord six days before his death.

After my husband died, I was determined not to let myself get caught up in the grief and fear of widowhood, because I needed to focus on surviving and taking care of my two children. My son John was already in college, but my daughter, Allison, was just nine years old when her dad passed away.

My coping mechanisms often found themselves at the breaking point. Despite my best attempts to ignore the emotional turmoil in my heart, it was still there. Stuffed under the surface, it had an inconvenient way of popping up and overwhelming me from time to time.

Rough Times

Between 1993 and 1997, my kids and I went through some really difficult times. I commuted a total of three hours a day to and from work. Every day was a tiring journey through back roads and small towns. This long commute meant leaving home in the dark and coming back in the dark.

That sort of schedule was terribly difficult, both on me and on John and Allison. After three years, I was physically and emotionally exhausted and realized something had to change. Although I didn't really know *how* things could change, I clearly couldn't keep up this grueling schedule.

After being widowed, I went almost five years without going on any dates. I reasoned that if God had another husband for me, it wouldn't be any problem for Him to bring someone into my life. I told my friends, "Instead of worrying about finding a relationship with a man, I'm going to simply trust God and build my relationship with Him."

During this time, some of my friends made dreadful choices in second marriages, so it wasn't hard for me to adopt the philosophy, "Better *no* husband than a *bad* husband!"

However, Allison was at the stage of life when she really wanted someone to be a dad for her. She frequently gave me not-so-subtle suggestions like, "Mom, let's face it. No one is asking you out. Are you sure you're wearing enough makeup?"

Allison became my constant companion. Even when I attended conferences, seminars, and training events, I took her with me whenever possible. I greatly enjoyed her company, and it helped insulate me from impulsively forming any new relationships.

In the spring of 1997, I signed up for an Israel tour in June. However, even though I had sent in my payment, in

May I got a real sense in my gut that I shouldn't go. Not really knowing why, I canceled.

Meanwhile, I received an invitation to attend a conference in Jacksonville, and this included an opportunity to meet with some intercessors who would be praying for the city. I passed the invitation on to my friend Gloria, thinking the conference might interest her.

Much to my surprise, Gloria called me soon afterwards and said, "The Lord told me to take you to that conference in Jacksonville. I'm going to pay your way, and this time you aren't supposed to take Allison with you!"

I had known Gloria for many years, and she had always been right on target with the things she heard from the Lord. So I hardly even questioned her words. And I sensed in my heart that it was important for me to go.

Little did I know that Thursday, June 12, 1997 was my date with destiny—the day that would change everything. Remember the story in Joshua 3 about the Israelites crossing the Jordan River, leaving the wilderness behind and entering the Promised Land? That's the kind of transformation God did in my heart that day. After years of quiet desperation as a worn out and wounded widow, I discovered a surprising life of "inexpressible and glorious joy" (1 Peter 1:8 NIV).

I had been a counselor in need of healing from the Wonderful Counselor. But I wasn't the only one being prepared for a date with destiny. The Lord had been bringing Dennis through some difficult—but amazing—transformations of his own.

part two

DENNIS' STORY:
a pastor at the end of his rope

chapter THREE
BEAUTY FOR ASHES

— by Dennis —

IN THE SPRING OF 1997, I was at the end of my rope. After years as a successful Pennsylvania pastor—bringing hope and healing to others—now my own life was in shambles.

Behind the scenes, I had struggled for years to salvage my troubled marriage. But finally the end came. My 25-year marriage ended in divorce, and I resigned as pastor of the church I had planted many years before.

I was devastated. Losing both my marriage and my ministry brought overwhelming confusion and pain.

What should I do now? I wondered. *I feel called to ministry, but how can I serve God in ministry again? Even if the Lord forgives me and restores me, will people ever accept a divorced pastor as their leader?*

I felt like a failure...a washed-up leader...a hopeless case for God to ever use again. I knew God hated divorce (Malachi 2:16), and the demons of hell were screaming their loudest that He hated *me* as well.

Yet in the midst of my pain, God spoke to me that He was bringing me into a year of jubilee and time of restoration. Despite my failed marriage, He hadn't given up on me. And one day a man of God singled me out of a crowd and encouraged me through Proverbs 24:16 (NASB): "A righteous man falls seven times, and rises again."

My situation stood in stark contrast with God's promises in Isaiah 61:

- At a time when I saw bad news on every side, the Lord promised "good tidings" (v. 1).

- After my years of endeavoring to heal people's broken lives, now the Lord wanted to heal my *own* broken heart (v. 1).

- Despite the trauma of losing my marriage and ministry, He wanted to give me liberty from captivity (v. 1).

- As I mourned and experienced the grief process, He promised to console me and give me comfort (vs. 2-3).

- Though my entire life was desolate and in ruins, He said He would rebuild me into His image (v. 4).

- And through it all, He offered me the "great exchange": beauty for ashes, the oil of joy for mourning, and the garment of praise for the spirit of heaviness (v. 3).

Despite such wonderful promises for deep healing and restoration, I was painfully aware that my life was a mess. So when I heard or read promises like this, it was hard not to conclude that the Lord was just "messing with me." It was difficult to imagine life free from my current emotional baggage.

I was a basket case…a candidate for a major overhaul. And even if God could *eventually* restore me, I was sure it would be 5, 10 or 15 years before I would be ready for ministry again.

But God had other plans…

Promises Amid Problems

For years I'd been intrigued by this description of Abraham in Hebrews 11:8: "By faith Abraham obeyed when he was called to go out to the place which he would receive as an inheritance. And he went out, *not knowing where he was going*."

It was bad enough that Abraham was called toward a destiny he didn't understand, but in order to obey God and receive his promised inheritance, he had to leave behind everything that was comfortable and familiar (Genesis 12:1-2). The Lord said he would end up in "a land that I will show you," but it would have been nice to know a little more detail!

Of course, we know now that the story had a happy ending. God fulfilled His promise: "I will bless you and make your name great; and you shall be a blessing."

Like Abraham, I was sensing God leading me to leave my comfort zone in Pennsylvania and venture out to new territory, both geographically and spiritually. But it was hard to be confident my story would have a happy ending. Yet, at times I heard God promising to bless me and make me a blessing again in ministry to others.

At one point, I distinctly heard Him promise to meet all my financial needs, even without needing to seek secular employment. However, with my ministry gone and only a few months of savings in my bank account, it was difficult to comprehend how the Lord would ever fulfill this.

Still hurt and confused, it wasn't easy to trust my inner sense of God's will. Yet somehow He enabled me to feel moments of hope that He truly *could* bring beauty out of my ashes.

Launching Out

Having no idea why, I was feeling an increasing desire to move to Charlotte, North Carolina. Giving me no details, the Lord impressed Jeremiah 29:7 on my heart as some sort of future assignment: "Seek the peace of the city where I have caused you to be carried away captive, and pray to the LORD for it; for in its peace you will have peace."

It would have been one thing if Charlotte was a place where I already had family or friends. A ready-made support system would have been nice at that point in my life.

However, I knew no one in Charlotte, and I had no plans for what I was to do when I arrived there. No family. No friends. No job. No ministry. Charlotte was no more than a point on the map to me. Yet in March 1997 I packed up a few belongings in my car and left for an uncertain future, hundreds of miles away from my roots.

What a strange sensation! I felt like a man without a country. I had lived for years in familiar surroundings. I drove the same route to work each day, got my hair cut at the same place, and used the same dry cleaners.

I had a great support system of friends in Pennsylvania. I knew all the other local pastors, and several of them had been dear friends for many years. My life had practically been on autopilot.

Yet while I enjoyed the stability and predictability of my Pennsylvania roots, I was aware that comfort zones can become coffins if we aren't willing to lay things down to follow God's call. I found myself in a position like the four lepers who asked themselves: "Why do we sit here until we die?" (2 Kings 7:3 NASB). Staying would mean eventual "death," while leaving in obedience to God would mean a new life.

But why Charlotte? I had never even visited this city I was planning to make my new home. I didn't know a soul there. And when friends asked for my new contact information, I couldn't even give them an address or phone number.

Was I just going crazy? I felt confused and alone as I approached the city I hoped would be my place of new beginnings.

Strange Signposts

Something extraordinary happened as I crossed into the Charlotte city limits. In a flash, my mind's eye saw a city map suddenly burst into flames, just like the Ponderosa map in the opening sequence of the popular Bonanza television series years ago.

This experience was both exciting and bewildering. Although it seemed an encouraging confirmation that the Lord had something special in mind for me in Charlotte, it also reminded me I had absolutely no idea what the future would hold there.

I've never been very good at following maps and directions. Not knowing my way around Charlotte, I drove straight through the city on I-77 and nearly ended up in South Carolina. Seeing exit 1, I realized I needed to get off the freeway immediately or else I'd be past Charlotte.

"Lead me, Lord!" I whispered a nervous prayer of both hope and desperation. Without any particular destination in mind, I turned onto the exit ramp and just kept driving. I knew of several churches in the area and wanted to find my church home before proceeding with other decisions.

Somehow, I ended up on South Polk Street on the southern edge of Charlotte. When I noticed a small metal building with children's playground equipment and cars parked outside, I decided to stop and ask directions to a local church with which I was familiar.

As I pulled into the parking lot, I noticed a man sitting in one of the cars. I rolled down my window, but before I could even get a word out, the man said, "Are you going to ask for directions? The Lord told me to wait in the car, because someone was going to ask me for directions, and I needed to be here!"

I was startled by the man's statement, but it also was tremendously encouraging. Immediately some of my feelings of aloneness left, and I was filled with reassurance that God was still very much with me. Although I felt completely lost in this strange new city, my Heavenly Father had everything under control. Some sort of wonderful plan had been mapped out for me, and I was stumbling upon it with each new twist and turn of the road.

After the man gave me directions to a church I'd heard about in Charlotte, I found a nearby hotel where I could spend the night before embarking again on my new adventure the following day. That night I tossed and turned in anticipation.

Surprising Open Doors

The next day was Saturday, and I drove to the church that man had given me directions to. I did not really expect it to be open, but I just wanted to make sure I could find it Sunday morning.

To my surprise, the building was open, and it turned out that an usher's meeting was taking place. I went inside and saw a bulletin board with notices of items for sale, students looking for Christian roommates, and apartments for rent.

I didn't have a lasting place to stay yet, and the hotel would be far too expensive for the long term. So I copied down a list of possibilities from the bulletin board, hoping to find a suitable Christian roommate and inexpensive rent.

Not wanting to use up minutes on my cell phone, I found a pay phone and began dialing the numbers for potential apartments. Much to my frustration, all the doors seemed closed. Some of the places had already been rented, and others were looking for a female roommate or a student in the ministry school. After one refusal after another, my list was pretty much exhausted.

I dialed one more number, and my heart sank as the woman on the other end of the line said, "No, I don't have anything."

However, the power of God suddenly flooded the phone booth, and I was astonished to hear her say, "Oh, my! Oh, my! Can I call you back in a minute?"

Later I discovered she had called a friend to pray, telling her, "Would you pray for me? I was talking to a man looking for a place to rent, and I told him a clear 'no.' But then I heard the Lord say, *Do something for this man!*"

After a few minutes, the woman called me back at the phone booth and said, "Can you meet me for lunch?" At lunch, she told me she had a condominium I could rent. God had told her to let me stay there rent free as long as I liked, if I was willing to sign a lease…for a dollar.

Her condo was fully furnished—including towels, bed sheets, silverware, dishes, pots and pans, and a washer and dryer. It even had a deck overlooking a beautiful lake! When I moved in few days later, I sat on the deck and cried at the goodness of God.

My life still seemed a mess, but the Lord was clearly moving. Like the earth is described in Genesis 1:2, I sometimes felt "formless and empty," and often "darkness was over the surface" of my life. However, in the midst of the chaos and confusion, "the Spirit of God was hovering."

Despite these signs of hope, I still couldn't help but wonder where the path would lead. Yes, I could see unmistakable signs God was blessing me, but could He truly make me a blessing to others again? And even though I was grateful He was beginning to heal my inner pain, it still was unfathomable that He could use me to bring deep relief to others in their distress.

Yet one day the dark clouds parted and a breakthrough came, suddenly changing everything.

chapter FOUR
RENDEZVOUS WITH DESTINY

by Dennis

MY ENTIRE CHRISTIAN LIFE, I had always been involved in a church, and that was my intention in Charlotte as well. But as you might imagine, this wasn't very easy.

In Pennsylvania, I had been a senior pastor...a leader...a minister...a counselor...a teacher. However, here I was in a new city, and no one knew me. I was a nobody—and a *divorced* nobody at that.

No one knew I had been in ministry, nor was I in any hurry to *let* them know. I was feeling fragile in my calling and uncertain about what my future ministry, if I had any, would look like.

Whenever I pondered involvement in the church I was attending in Charlotte, my mind was flooded with troubling questions. *Would the church leadership feel threatened when they found out I had been a pastor? And what would they think when they learned I had been divorced? Would they ever allow a divorced person to be involved in ministry?*

Instead of fretting about whether I would be accepted or not, I decided to set my heart on finding ways to serve.

And recalling the scripture God had given me about praying for the city, I figured the best place to start was volunteering for the intercessory prayer team. It seemed like the safest and most inconspicuous place of service I could find.

It turned out that many of the intercessors were planning to go to Jacksonville, Florida to pray for a big conference there. Without any source of income, my meager savings was diminishing daily, so I was pretty squeamish about making a trip to Florida. It seemed to make little sense, yet somehow I felt I was supposed to go.

Meanwhile, the pastor took me up on my offer to help out in any area where help was needed. He asked me to join eight other people in preparing 3,000 information packets for the upcoming conference. It was a big project, expected to take us the better part of a day.

While we were preparing the packets, one person suggested it would help pass the time if we went around the room and shared our testimonies. I inwardly groaned, feeling much too raw from recent events to want to share with a group of strangers. But I figured I just had to make the best of it.

It caught my attention when a young man shared that he was planning a cruise a few years prior, and God told him he would meet his wife on the cruise: "You will know she is the one," the Lord supposedly said, "because she will pray for you and then ask you to pray for her!"

I thought this was a hilarious story. After all, believers pray for one another all the time, so how could that possibly stand out as unusual?

However, as I smugly chuckled to myself, the power of God hit me so hard that my knees almost buckled. To my amazement, the Lord distinctly said, "The same thing is going to happen to you, Dennis!"

"Wait a minute here," I silently protested. "Lord, this is *much* too soon to contemplate remarriage."

Despite my initial misgivings, I recognized God's unmistakable voice. After wrestling with this for a while, I finally resolved it in my heart: "OK, Lord, maybe I would be open to consider marriage again five or ten years down the road. But certainly no sooner." Even with this faint openness to remarriage, I added one final requirement: "Father, there's no way I want to get married again unless my wife is my best friend." I had seen enough troubled marriages over the years to know that couples rarely survived the difficulties of life unless they had first become best friends.

Just a few days later, I drove down to Jacksonville to attend the conference. Little did I know that God was orchestrating a rendezvous with destiny. Expecting just to intercede and serve quietly behind the scenes, I was stunned when Thursday, June 12, 1997 became—as Jen described it earlier—***the day that changed everything***.

—part three—
OUR STORIES INTERSECT:
making all things new

chapter **FIVE**
THE SOUND OF A VOICE

by Dr. Jen

EARLY ON THE MORNING of June 12, I (Jen) waited on the side porch of my house in Waycross, Georgia and my friend Gloria pulled into the driveway. We were taking an unfamiliar route north of Jacksonville, and Gloria was uncertain about the driving time to our destination. So we loaded the car as quickly as we could and sped off for our destination near the beach on the east side of Jacksonville.

Gloria and I arrived barely in time for the first session in the sanctuary, and it was too late to go looking for the intercessors' meeting room. As soon as the meeting concluded, though, we found someone with a staff badge who led us to the intercessors.

About 90 intercessors were meeting in a large room near the fellowship hall. During the afternoon meeting, the leaders asked for 15 volunteers to stay in a back room and pray throughout the conference, even though this would cause them to miss the main meetings.

Well, I wanted to hear the speakers, but Gloria immediately volunteered both of us for the back room. So when we came back to the church that evening after dinner, we went straight to the prayer room.

"She Sounds Like Me"

Someone suggested we pray for one another before interceding for the conference and the city of Jacksonville. Dennis later said that as people were praying for each other's personal needs, he overheard me praying for one of the other intercessors. Once again, he was struck by a sudden surge of the power of God and his knees almost buckled again. Before even turning to see who it was that was praying, he thought, "She sounds like me when she prays!"

"Hmmm," he wondered, "What does it even mean that 'she sounds like me'?" At that, Dennis looked to see who he had heard. He turned toward me and our eyes met.

We spoke briefly, and I felt impressed to pray for him, so I asked if that was alright. After I prayed a little while, he acted like he was going to walk away, so I exclaimed, "Wait. I haven't finished praying yet!"

Dennis later explained that he was completely overwhelmed with everything going on. And he couldn't help but remember the story he heard a few days earlier of the couple who met on a cruise. The young man sharing the testimony had quoted the Lord as saying, "She will pray for you and then ask you to pray for her." But since the second part of the sentence didn't happen that night, Dennis tried to pass off the whole thing as coincidence.

During that whole evening, I kept hearing Dennis' voice as he prayed. I didn't particularly notice anything else about him, but his voice echoed in my ears and touched my heart. Sometimes the unguarded sound of a person's voice reveals their heart and core identity, and that's what I felt about Dennis as the intercessors prayed that night.

Although you might think matters of love and attraction are strange subjects for scientific study, they're actually hot topics for research right now. A scientist studying the science of romance was told in an interview: "I knew, when I first heard that voice, that he was for me." The scientist concluded that "the music of the voice [was] perhaps a better indication of a man's soul [than physical appearance]."[1]

When I read this scientist's observation, my thoughts instantly went back to the weekend when Dennis and I first met. As he prayed, the sound of his voice somehow resonated deep within my heart just as, Dennis said, my voice did with him.

Can We Be Friends?

The next morning we all went into the sanctuary, where the first two rows had been reserved for the intercessors. Gloria came in early and found a seat, but it turned out that there were two more intercessors than there were reserved seats. Dennis and I were the last to arrive, so there were no reserved seats left. Instead, we found two seats together near the back of the room and had an opportunity to talk a bit.

When the session was over, Dennis asked if I would like to go somewhere for lunch. My thoughts raced. I hadn't been out with any man for almost five years, and I was in no hurry to change that. I had told the Lord I was going to run from men, but I gave Him permission to stop me if He ever wanted to bring me another husband.

Rather than completely accept Dennis' invitation, I said I hadn't been out with anyone since my husband's death, but I would find my friend Gloria and the three of us could go as a group. We drove to a nearby Quincy's buffet, and when we found a table several other people from the conference asked if they could join us.

Ever since the evening before, I had been thinking, "I should have asked Dennis to pray for me!" So I leaned toward him at our table and said, "When we get back to the church this afternoon, I want you to pray for me."

I wasn't prepared for his reaction! First, Dennis' face turned white. Then he pushed his chair back from the table, turned to the side, and doubled over. I was so perplexed that I kept asking, "What's wrong?! What did I say?"

At first he didn't want to tell me, but I wouldn't let his overreaction go without some kind of explanation. Later, he divulged that my probing caused him to pray in silent desperation, "Help, Lord! What am I supposed to say *now*?" The second part of the young couple's testimony, "...and then ask you to pray for her," was happening just like the Lord had spoken to Dennis only a few days before. Dennis later said, "I was completely overwhelmed with astonishment that Jen was my wife-to-be!"

Dennis remembered how he had qualified the thought of remarriage as being the union of best friends. So he told me the story of the couple and their testimony of praying for each other on the cruise. But he watered down the story's application to us, saying the Lord said He would send him a friend. Well, that melted my heart. "Of course I'll be your friend!" I assured him.

My First How-To

Later that afternoon, we discovered that the prayer room was locked, so Dennis, Gloria and I sat on the carpet while the cleaning staff vacuumed around us. That's when Dennis prayed for me the very first time.

As we closed our eyes to pray, I learned my first how-to lesson from Dennis. He told me to open my heart, which confused me at first. Thinking of the physical heart, it took me a while to get his point.

But when he gave me a little more instruction, I began to understand. He told me to put my hand on my belly, and yield there to Christ in my heart. He quoted the word of Jesus in John 7:38, "He that believeth on me, as the scripture hath said, out of his belly shall flow rivers of living water."

I had always thought my spiritual heart was where my physical heart was, even though the Bible clearly said *belly*. Never before had I heard anyone tell someone else to yield their heart, where to yield, or how to yield. But as I attempted to cooperate, he encouraged me, "There, you're doing it."

At the same time, I could *feel* the difference inside my heart. I don't remember exactly what we prayed about, but looking back, I can see that he led me through some how-to's for healing of the heart.

I still didn't catch the full significance of what I was learning. However, it was obvious that Dennis had a unique anointing and spiritual authority, and he was teaching principles that were entirely new to me.

"Step Into Your Destiny!"

By mid-afternoon the intercessors had started trickling back to the church, and someone unlocked the prayer room. Since it wasn't yet time for the meeting to begin, people milled around and talked up and down the hall and in the room itself.

I was in the hall talking to someone, and Dennis had gone into the room. The first day of the conference, Dennis had seen someone he knew in the audience, and they caught each other's eye. They had not seen each other since then, and she came looking for him in the prayer room to say hello.

Without warning, she burst into the room, came over to Dennis and exclaimed, "Have you met anyone?" That shook him, so he tried to make a joke and change the subject.

But she stopped him mid-sentence. "No, wait!" she demanded. "I'm speaking to you as an intercessor, not as a friend. Come out here into the hall."

At that, she grabbed Dennis' arm and pulled him to the door. Then she pointed at me down the hall. "When I was walking down the hall I could see you…married to *her*!"

At the very same time, the intercessor I was talking to reached out and clasped my hands. Drawing an imaginary line on the floor with her foot, she pulled me across the line and said, "The Lord is saying to you, 'Step into your destiny, Jen!'"

By now Dennis was on emotional overload. Significant praying was impossible. So he walked over to the sanctuary door and peered at the musicians on stage. The usher standing near the door looked at him and queried, "Are you looking for your wife…the one with the white top and blue print skirt?" He described my outfit exactly.

Unable to respond coherently, Dennis inhaled deeply and closed the door. This was just too much to take in at one time!

The Big Meltdown

Remember the story I told in the first chapter about the emotional meltdown of a young woman named Amanda? This happened the following afternoon, when the intercessors were praying for those in Jacksonville who were held captive to fear or intimidation.

Suddenly, Amanda collapsed to the floor. Dennis went over to pray with her, while the rest of us were stunned into inaction. Yet I was close enough to see what was taking place and hear how Dennis was praying for her.

He guided her in praying through multiple areas of fears and hurts. One at a time, he addressed each new area that came up. Only after she felt true relief did Dennis move on to another issue. Remarkably, it just took a few minutes to address each area of fear, but Amanda could tell she was experiencing a real inner transformation.

All the intercessors were gathered around, watching with amazement. I was blown away by how much emotional pain was dealt with and how fast the relief came. I had seen lots of counseling and psychological therapy over the years, but nothing like this.

"Wow!" I thought. "This is the answer everyone is yearning for!" I felt like I had just witnessed something as monumental as the cure for "emotional cancer."

This was the missing ingredient needed to heal the wounded people and troubled church. Here, at last, was the secret for healing emotional pain quickly.

Stunned by this rapid, visible transformation, the person in charge of the meeting stood with mouth wide open and incredulously asked the pastor, "Who *are* you?"

chapter SIX
FROM PRAYER PARTNERS TO LIFE PARTNERS
by Dr. Jen

AFTER DENNIS INTERVENED to bring Amanda quick relief during her emotional meltdown, things also moved forward very quickly in our relationship. By the time the sun set and evening came, we were together every possible moment.

Only days earlier, we had just been strangers volunteering to pray at a conference. Along the way, God led us to pray for each other, which was a significant step.

However, in record time, the Lord took us from being strangers, to being prayer partners, to an amazing peace and excitement that He might be bonding us together as partners for life. My friend Gloria said later that she was starting to feel like a chaperone for madly in love high school kids.

As the days unfolded, it became clear that this was the first step in God fulfilling His promise to make "all things new" (Revelation 21:5) in our lives. I call it "the day that changed everything," because that's exactly what the Lord did—He changed *everything* for me and Dennis. Seeing a counselor who needed healing and a pastor at the end of his rope, He looked down with His incredible mercy to bring us hope and healing.

The conference was over Saturday night, so Sunday morning Dennis drove back to Charlotte and I returned home to Waycross. However, that evening Dennis called me and we talked for five hours! As I sat talking with him, Allison sat down at the kitchen table and watched in amazement. This was quite a strange event she was witnessing. Her mom was actually talking with a *man*!

Dennis called again the following night, and this time he decided to tell me the *whole* story about the young couple who met on the cruise, prayed for each other, and were married a short time later. This time he admitted that the Lord had used the word *wife*.

The phone calls were wonderful, but the tension of not seeing each other was becoming too much to bear. Waycross was a six-hour drive from Charlotte, but Dennis left early the next day and arrived at my house by noon.

Gloria and her husband invited Dennis to stay with them while he was in town, and he ended up staying for a whole week. We talked nonstop, and I was thrilled to get to know him. We had the same heart in so many areas, and we already were openly talking about marriage. At the end of the week, Dennis had to return to Charlotte, but Allison and I made plans to drive to Charlotte for the Fourth of July.

Although we wanted to get married as soon as possible, I knew I would need to work at first. So I began checking on job openings in Charlotte. Even before Allison and I visited the area, I had three interviews lined up.

Allison and I reserved a room at the Days Inn. In addition to having a great time seeing the area, I was thrilled by how well Allison hit it off with Dennis. One highlight was when he took her roller skating, skated with her, and taught her how to skate backwards.

New Job, New Home, New Life

By the end of the week in Charlotte, I had three job offers. So now the three of us went house hunting. I had a large old house in Waycross, with a lot of furniture, so we checked out real estate with my furniture in mind.

For several days, we didn't see anything that would even remotely work. The houses were too dark, too small, too poorly designed, or too far from town. There was always something.

So the three of us drove to look around in nearby Rock Hill, South Carolina, and we pulled into a fast food parking lot to pray. "Lord, please help!" Time was running out, and Allison and I would be returning to Waycross soon.

We pulled out of the parking lot, drove a few blocks, then felt led to pull into a neighborhood near Winthrop University. It was an older section of town, and huge oak trees formed a canopy over the roads. We made another turn, and there was a grey ranch-style house with a "For Sale by Owner" sign in front. So we parked on the street, got out, and rang the doorbell.

An attractive woman answered the door but asked us to give her about 30 minutes to straighten up the house before giving us a tour. We ate a bite of lunch, then drove back and rang the doorbell again.

The exterior of the house was simple, but the interior was quite charming. It had a large living room and dining room, as well as a knotty pine-paneled study with built-in bookshelves. The breakfast nook had a lovely stained-glass window. A very large master suite had been added at the rear, and there was another stained-glass window in the master bathroom.

I was walking with the owner, Janice, as she pointed out the various features, but Allison was walking behind us. She was holding onto Dennis' arm and whispering into his ear, repeatedly saying, "This is it. This is the one! Do you think mom knows that this is it? Should we tell her?"

Janice was a school teacher and was hoping to sell her house and move into a new home by the time the new school year started. She let me sign a contract contingent on my house selling, and agreed to hold it for two weeks.

Allison and I said goodbye to Dennis and drove back to Waycross. I spread the word that my house was for sale and had a buyer in just two days…for cash! I was so happy I could call Janice and finalize the purchase of our new home in Rock Hill.

Plans and Purpose

God has wonderful plans for our lives (Jeremiah 29:11), and it was great to see all the pieces come together for my new job and new home. The next step was to plan our wedding and moving arrangements.

Even with details like these, we sensed God's favor and guidance. As Proverbs 16:9 (NLT) says, "We can make our plans, but the Lord determines our steps." Dennis and I were married informally August 6, 1997, but then we had a formal wedding ceremony on August 30.

As Allison and I prepared to leave Waycross behind, Dennis was concerned about how Allison would feel about leaving her school and friends. But as she buckled her seatbelt to depart for her new life in Charlotte, she turned to Dennis and said, "Thank goodness you are taking us out of this one-horse town!"

When we arrived back in Charlotte, I was delighted to meet Dennis' landlady, who had generously let him stay in her condo for one dollar. She declared when she saw us, "Listen, you two, God didn't bring you together just for your own pleasure. He brought you together for a *Kingdom purpose*."

Her word of encouragement was so true. And to think it all started with two broken people who first were intercessors and prayer partners. God used "the sound of a voice" to bring us together to obey *His* voice and reflect His glory.

END NOTES

[1] Doidge, N. (2007). *The Brain that Changes Itself*. New York, NY: Penguin Group (USA) Inc. 101.

part four
DRN DISCOVERED

chapter SEVEN
HITTING BOTTOM, FINDING FORGIVENESS

by Dennis

I WAS RAISED AS A CATHOLIC and went to parochial school from kindergarten through second grade. As a young Catholic, I struggled with the whole concept of confession and forgiveness. Between visits to the confessional, I found myself tormented by the guilt of my sins and apparent inability to change my behavior.

Before I even made it home from the confessional, I found myself plagued by unkind, selfish or lustful thoughts, and this led me to an inevitable conclusion: The only way I could ever make it into heaven was to be hit by a car as soon as I had confessed.

I also was troubled by the realization that I never told the whole truth in the confessional. Full honesty would cause me to undergo too much penance, so I did everything possible to sugarcoat my sins. However, this didn't really work either. For even if I received forgiveness, it would be based on an incomplete accounting of my misdeeds.

The result of this never-ending cycle was that although I craved forgiveness, I never really experienced it. Having a true relationship with God in this life seemed impossible, let alone making it through the pearly gates after I died.

Looking for Relief

I believe everyone is looking for relief—deep relief—from some kind of inner torment or dysfunction. People pursue different remedies to "medicate their pain," but the result is always the same: a downward spiral of even *greater* pain and emptiness.

In my case, I looked to drugs to give me relief and numb my emotional agony. It's ironic that people describe drugs as giving them a "high," because they usually end up, like me, at rock bottom.

By this time, I had a wife and infant son, and I had to rely on welfare to support our family. My addictions, bad attitudes, and utter helplessness without God had crippled my ability to be the provider God intended.

At last, I reached my "pigpen moment" (see Luke 15:15-16 if you're not familiar with what I mean). Our baby was sick and needed medicine. I had been given a Medicaid prescription, but it was tossed into the trash by accident. In desperation, I found myself standing in a dumpster, digging through the trash so our son could have the medicine he needed.

Friends and acquaintances drove by honking and waving as they recognized me standing red-faced in the dumpster. It was a moment of total humiliation—but also a much-needed wake up call.

Born Again

Many years later, several Christians told me I'd been so wild they thought it was useless to bother praying for my salvation. They explained that they had focused their prayers on people who seemed to have more of a chance! However, *someone* must have been praying, because at age 29 I finally experienced God's gift of salvation and was born again during a Christian television program.

Within the first year, I had such unusual and dramatic spiritual experiences that I was thrown onto the local Christian TV circuit to share my testimony. Even though I was a complete novice in the Christian life, people marveled at how God had so rapidly transformed my life.

Although the Lord taught me many wonderful things in those early days as a new convert, I particularly fell in love with forgiveness. My family line was known for unforgiveness, and I remembered hearing my mother say with great pride, "I *never* forgive and I *never* forget!"

My mother's sister was the same way. When I was a teen, I didn't want to dance with my cousin because she was taller than me. When my mother asked why I refused to dance her with at a particular dance, I answered, "She's just too big!" Well, my mother made the mistake of sharing this explanation with her sister, saying I thought her daughter was too big. Because of this seemingly insignificant event, my aunt was so offended that the two sisters didn't speak to one another for 14 years after that.

What a silly mess! My mom's sister was offended, and my mom was offended that her sister was offended! All because of a misunderstood statement by a teen about not dancing with his cousin.

A Forgiveness Lifestyle

Jesus paid a tremendous price to give His greatest gift to mankind: the gift of forgiveness. This amazing gift is our ticket to freedom…the bringer of peace…the heart healer and balm for strained relationships.

To my great surprise and relief, no more trips to the confessional were necessary to provide my forgiveness! I learned from 1 John 1:9 and other passages that I could go directly to Jesus and receive forgiveness—any time, any place: "If we confess our sins, He is faithful and just to forgive us our sins and to cleanse us from ALL unrighteousness."

I made up my mind that I was going to live a lifestyle of forgiveness. I learned to immediately *receive* forgiveness when I sinned and *extend* forgiveness when people wronged me. And I discovered that whenever I felt negative emotions, my peace could be restored through receiving God's forgiveness or deciding to forgive Him, myself or others.

Although I fell in love with the whole concept of forgiveness, I initially encountered one significant problem when I began to put it into practice. I found that I had so many impure thoughts, bad attitudes, and offenses that I was either forgiving or receiving forgiveness all day long. Forgiveness was fantastic, but it was taking up all my time!

I began to wonder how I could ever get any work done and still manage to live in forgiveness. However, I made up my mind that I was going to do this anyway.

Fortunately, things soon got better. I was relieved to discover that the times between my "forgiveness episodes" were getting farther and farther apart. The practice of forgiveness was actually changing me on the inside, gradually transforming my thoughts, attitudes and actions.

Knowing God

Growing up on the tough Chicago streets, I had learned the art of scowling to intimidate people and make them keep their distance. This "street sense" was simply a matter of self-preservation. Like Chicago gang members, I had begun to use anger as a wall of defense.

But now my countenance was radically different. Instead of anger, I felt and projected intense joy most of the time. In fact, I smiled so much that I earned the nickname "smiley." Thankfully, I was living in Pennsylvania at that point, because my beaming smiles would have gotten me beaten up in Chicago.

One of my early lessons was that I could perceive God's presence when I spent time with Him. My prayer times weren't focused on asking God for things, but simply on enjoying my relationship with Him. This was much more than just following a method or philosophy—I was communing with a real Person!

I also found that, just as in a relationship with another human being, the more time I spent with the Lord, the better I got to know Him. I began to understand His likes and dislikes, the inner sound of His voice, the gentle touch of His love and pleasure, and the nuances of His personality.

The verse of scripture which most perfectly described the longings of my heart to know and commune with God was Philippians 3:10 in the Amplified Bible:

> *[For my determined purpose is] that I may know Him [that I may progressively become more deeply and intimately acquainted with Him, perceiving and*

recognizing and understanding the wonders of His Person more strongly and more clearly] . . .

Paul's words here are not to be taken as just the experience of an elite group of super-spiritual Christians. No, this is meant to be the normal life of a believer—pressing on to know the Lord better each day.

In the School of the Spirit

One of the most important lessons I learned in my early days as a Christian was discernment. Through the Scriptures and His Holy Spirit, God was revealing Himself to me as my loving Heavenly Father. I discovered that there were numerous counterfeits of God's presence, and I needed an ability to discern which spiritual experiences were authentic.

People responsible for detecting counterfeit money are trained to discern what real currency looks like, and I found that the same principle applies to the spiritual realm. I set my heart on knowing God's loving nature so intimately that I wouldn't be fooled by imitations.

I learned that the nature of God is always loving, patient and pure. Even when we need His rod of correction, we can sense that all of heaven's love is behind it.

I soon became so acclimated to a loving, heavenly environment that I developed an antipathy for anything that blocked my inner sense of God's presence. The more I became acquainted with the reality of God, the more I felt an aversion to any negative emotion which disturbed my peace with Him. And the Lord taught me that forgiveness always brought me back to that amazing sense of peace.

God was personally taking me to the school of the Holy Spirit each day, instructing me in the intimate language and unique whisperings of the Spirit. I found that when the Lord awakened me at night to pray, it felt as gentle as the brush of a feather across my cheek. In time I learned to be obedient even to these gentle promptings.

Surprising Lessons

Some of the Holy Spirit's lessons surprised me. For example, it was puzzling at first that when the Lord quickened a scripture verse and I started talking to Him about it, the Spirit's anointing diminished. God explained, "You don't have anything worthwhile to say unless you first have *heard* something."

Isaiah 50:4 (AMP) teaches this very thing—that if we're going to speak a timely word to someone, we must first learn to hear God's voice "as one who is taught":

> *[The Servant of God says] The Lord God has given Me the tongue of a disciple and of one who is taught, that I should know how to speak a word in season to him who is weary. He wakens Me morning by morning, He wakens My ear to hear as a disciple [as one who is taught].*

I also learned that when God speaks, we need to truly absorb His words and make them a reality in our lives. If we're too eager to share what we've heard, our message is only information, not revelation.

This means we must learn how to listen and *wait* in the presence of the Lord:

> *Those who wait on the LORD Shall renew their strength; They shall mount up with wings like eagles,*

They shall run and not be weary, They shall walk and not faint (Isaiah 40:31).

I discovered that one of the great benefits of waiting was that I became aware of God's constant presence, and I paid attention when I felt any change or diminishing of the anointing. Whenever I sensed any change, I asked questions like this: "God, did I do or say something wrong?" or "Lord, I felt a quickening in my spirit when I thought about going to the bookstore. Does that mean You want me to go there?"

I *loved* to experience God's presence! And I became increasingly sensitive to avoid any thought, word or action that would hinder my relationship with Him.

But it wasn't enough to just experience God during my prayer times. I wanted to take the same sense of His presence with me *all day long*. I learned that I experienced His presence in different "emotions"—sometimes as a deep peace, and at other times as unspeakable joy. But there always was an awareness of His awesome holiness and love.

Learning From Brother Lawrence

Although God had put me in His personalized school of the Holy Spirit, He also sent me helpful mentors at various points in my journey. Some of these were believers who modeled the Christian life for me—but others were great men and women of God who "mentored" me through their writings or biographies.

Brother Lawrence, who lived from 1614 to 1691, was a monk in a Carmelite monastery in Paris. After he died, his letters were compiled into a book called *The Practice of the Presence of God.* It became one of the most popular Christian books of all time, among both Catholics and Protestants alike. Throughout the centuries, Brother Lawrence has been often quoted by such great Christian leaders as John Wesley and A.W. Tozer.

This humble monk who lived hundreds of years ago became a tremendous example for me. He sought to spend his entire life in unceasing adoration of God in every thought, word and action. Loving God became the theme and purpose of his life. Even while engaging in the mundane chores and activities of life, Brother Lawrence sought to glorify God and experience His presence. He didn't try to accomplish any great thing—he simply sought to live in love.

Brother Lawrence stood out among his peers because of his Christ-like example. He gained a reputation for living in such intimacy with God that he constantly experienced deep and profound peace.

For him, prayer wasn't just something to cross off a "To Do" list. Instead of being something he *did*, prayer was Someone he loved. Brother Lawrence modeled the kind of life I craved, a life of prayer without ceasing (1 Thessalonians 5:17).

Discerning the Spiritual Atmosphere

Have you ever noticed how easy it is to be influenced by the unpleasant environments around you? Perhaps you've felt nervous while watching another person who was nervous when speaking before a crowd. Or maybe you've felt yourself getting angry when surrounded by angry people.

This experience of picking up the spiritual environment around us is actually a form of discernment. It's an example of being sensitive to the atmosphere of the world around us.

As I became more acclimated to experiencing of God's loving nature, I began to fiercely dislike anything that interrupted my peace. And I found that while I honed my awareness of the presence of God, I also developed a great sensitivity to other people. When they were nervous, angry or hurting, I was able to pick up their emotions quite easily.

However, in my early days as a believer, I still had plenty of hurts, wounds and rejections. Because of this, it often triggered my own pain and insecurities when I felt the pain of others. So I begged the Lord to take away this new sensitivity: "Lord, I have way too much of my *own* pain. I certainly don't want to feel the pain of others!"

A pivotal moment occurred during the first year after my conversion. I had been asked to share my testimony at a small meeting. But when I went up on the stage to speak, I was hit out of the blue by an overwhelming wave of fear and shame. I was so gripped by these toxic emotions that I couldn't say a word. I just walked off the platform, and the worship leader filled in the gap and gave her testimony instead.

What a humiliating turn of events! I loved Jesus with all my heart, and was having rich experience with Him in prayer. What was wrong with me?

As soon as I got home, I fell on my knees in prayer and cried out, "Lord, I don't understand what happened. Where did this come from?"

Instantly, I saw myself as a nine-year-old boy with clenched fists, hating himself for being a bed-wetter. Two decades from that painful time in my life, I felt the hatred and shame just as if it happened yesterday.

I had always known it was wrong to hate other people. However, now I was seeing how wrong and harmful it was to hate myself.

As I humbled myself in prayer, I experienced the Lord washing away my feelings of shame and removing the self-hatred from my heart. As soon as I was cleansed of these negative emotions, my heart was flooded with the incredible love and peace of God!

I realized I had learned a profound secret, important not only for my own Christian life but for countless others who needed similar hope and healing. Starting with this pivotal incident, the Lord began to show me how bad emotions interrupt our ability to practice His presence. As I learned to deal with these negative emotions, I found that I was able to connect with the love nature of God once again.

Somehow it surprised me that whenever I invited God to come and touch an area in my heart, He really showed up to do it! I discovered that Bible principles truly work, and Jesus does what He says He will do. God is always willing to save, and He is always willing to sanctify.

Often we tell lost people they should open the door of their heart to Jesus to receive His salvation, and that is true. But now I was discovering I could choose to continuously open my heart to Him. Jesus says in Revelation 3:20:

Behold, I stand at the door and knock. If anyone hears My voice and opens the door, I will come in to him and dine with him, and he with Me.

Of course, in the original context of this passage, Jesus is speaking to *Christians*, not unbelievers. His offer of intimacy and freedom is made to *anyone* who hears His voice, and that is good news for each of us.

As the Lord taught me to walk in forgiveness and cherish His love and peace, it became apparent that this must become a way of life for me, not just a series of random events. I had been equipped with some powerful "God Tools"—practical how-to's for walking moment by moment in the Lord's presence. Now I learned to apply those tools in my daily life and would one day begin to teach these same principles to others.

These foundational experiences form the basis for Deep Relief Now. In the following chapters, you'll learn how to begin applying these secrets in your own life. As your life begins to radiate new peace and joy, get ready for people to ask what has happened to you. When they ask, "Where did you learn this?" make sure to buy them a copy of this book!

part five
THE POWER OF SIMPLE PRAYER

chapter **EIGHT**
LOCATION, LOCATION, LOCATION

by Dennis

IN THE PREVIOUS SECTIONS of this book, Dr. Jen and I shared some our own story. Both of us have experienced what it's like to be broken people, in need of Deep Relief through God's healing touch. Although we both were believers before the Lord showed us the principles of DRN, our spiritual growth was stunted by inner turmoil and emotional pain.

Sharing our story was just a prelude to what this book is really about: Showing you how to experience Deep Relief in your own life. As the book unfolds, we'll also be sharing some brief stories of how God has already used DRN to quickly transform countless others.

If you're already a Christian, you may be asking yourself at this point, "Why haven't I already been healed of my emotional pain? I pray, read my Bible, and attend church—yet my emotional baggage never seems to go away."

That's a great question, and you're not alone in asking it. Some people don't even realize that God is *able* to give them Deep Relief from their inner pain. Others have adopted the misguided notion that the Lord is not *willing* to heal them—choosing to let them struggle throughout life with psychological hang-ups as some sort of "cross to bear." However, in many cases, we believe God's healing touch is possible, but we simply don't know how to access it.

When I first met Jen, I could tell right away that she was very intelligent and well educated. She was an intellectual, used to living her life in the cognitive realm—in her head, rather than her heart.

Because Jen approached life primarily through mental analysis, she struggled to understand what was happening when she prayed or worshiped. Most of her prayer life was a matter of prayer lists and petitions, but this didn't result in true intimacy with the Lord.

Through her analytical approach, Jen was able to learn many facts *about* God, but her mindset wasn't very conducive to a close *relationship* with Him. The relational aspect of her spiritual life was more accidental than purposeful. Although she avidly read books about the prayer lives of great men and women of God, she was starving for more of God's reality in her own life.

The first thing I had to teach Jen was what had happened when she asked Jesus into her heart, and how to continue to encounter Him in prayer. I think you will be greatly helped by this vital first lesson of DRN.

What Prayer Really Entails

God wants to be Lord of our entire life, not just our "spiritual" life. Since He made us thinking, willing, feeling beings, He wants us to let Him be Lord of our thoughts, choices, and emotions.

Throughout the Scriptures, we're told…

- God's thoughts are higher than our thoughts (Isaiah 55:8-9, Romans 11:33-34).

- His will is superior to the choices we would make on our own (Proverbs 14:12, Proverbs 3:5-7).

- His love is superior to our carnal emotions (1 Corinthians 13, 1 John 2:15-17).

Some people treat prayer much the same as little children who send their gift requests to Santa Claus at Christmas. Without seeking any relationship, they expectantly mail their letters to Santa at the North Pole.

Prayer is meant to be a lot more than this. In prayer we give the Lord access to our innermost being—our heart—so He heals us, transforms us, and gives us revelation and guidance. There are deep places in the human heart that we all tend to hide and cover up through fear and denial. But God uses His Word, His Spirit, and wise counselors to shine the light of healing:

> *Counsel in the heart of man is like water in a deep well, but a man of understanding draws it out (Proverbs 20:5 AMP).*

After we got married, Jen asked me to disciple her in prayer. She was still working a secular job for that first year, but after she got home we ate dinner and spent time praying together. Out of these prayer times, we developed the How-To's we now teach others.

Have you ever thought about how significant it was that the disciples asked Jesus, "Lord, teach us to pray"? (Luke 11:1). There's no record of them ever asking Him the How-To's of healing the sick, casting out demons, or teaching the Word, but they wanted to know how to pray. Why? Because they saw this was the key to everything else Jesus did.

The Location of the Heart

Many believers are confused about the difference between their head and their heart. They wonder if prayer is simply a matter of having the right thoughts in their head, or whether there should also be some other component—a matter of the heart and emotions.

During the 18th century, a French philosopher named Blaise Pascal once wrote, "There is a God-shaped hole in the heart of every man which cannot be filled by any created thing, but only by God the Creator."

So, exactly where *is* a person's heart? If Jesus truly wants to come and live in our heart, what does that mean?

In order to answer this important question, let's go to the Bible. In the Old Testament and New Testament alike, Hebrew and Greek words describing the *belly* or *bowels* are regularly translated "heart" in English. For example, in John 7:38 (NKJV), the Greek word for belly is rendered as heart, but the KJV provides a more literal translation: "He that believeth on me, as the scripture hath said, out of his **belly** shall flow rivers of living water."

The Message paraphrase says it this way: "Rivers of living water will brim and spill **out of the depths** of anyone who believes in me this way." So the heart is described as "the depths" of our being, or as David said, the "innermost being" and "hidden part" (Psalm 51:6). The Bible has a lot more to say about the location and function of the heart:

- **The heart is the seat of emotion.**

*Whoso hath this world's good, and seeth his brother have need, and shutteth up his **BOWELS OF COMPASSION** from him, how dwelleth the love of God in him? (1 John 3:17 KJV).*

- **The door of the heart can either open or shut.**

*Whoever has this world's goods, and sees his brother in need, and **SHUTS UP HIS HEART** from him, how does the love of God abide in him? (1 John 3:17 NKJV).*

- **The anointing of the Holy Spirit is released and flows from the heart (KJV "belly").**

*He who believes in Me, as the Scripture has said, **OUT OF HIS HEART WILL FLOW RIVERS** of living water (John 7:38 NKJV).*

*Above all else, guard your **HEART**, for it is the **WELLSPRING** of life (Proverbs 4:23 NIV).*

*Whoever drinks of the water that I shall give him will never thirst. But the water that I shall give him will become in him a **FOUNTAIN** of water springing up into everlasting life (John 4:14).*

- **Wounds of the heart are located in the belly.**

*The words of a talebearer are as **WOUNDS**, and they go down into the **INNERMOST PARTS** of the **BELLY** (Proverbs 18:8 KJV).*

- **The spirit of man is in the belly or heart.**

*The **SPIRIT OF MAN** is the lamp of the Lord, searching all the **INWARD PARTS** of the **BELLY** [heart] (Proverbs 20:27 KJV).*

*The spirit of a man is the lamp of the Lord, searching all the **INNER DEPTHS** of his **HEART** (Proverbs 20:27 KJV; footnote: Literally "the rooms of the belly").*

Within our heart, we locate the following:

- the seat of grief: John 14:1; Romans 9:2; 2 Corinthians 2:4
- joy: John 16:22; Ephesians 5:19
- the desires: Matthew 5:28; 2 Peter 2:14
- the affections: Luke 24:32; Acts 21:13
- the perceptions: John 12:40; Ephesians 4:18
- the thoughts: Matthew 9:4; Hebrews 4:12
- the understanding: Matthew 13:15; Romans 1:21
- the reasoning powers: Mark 2:6; Luke 24:38
- the imagination: Luke 1:51
- conscience: Acts 2:37; 1 John 3:20
- the intentions: Heb 4:12; 1 Peter 4:1
- purpose: Acts 11:23; 2 Corinthians 9:7
- the will: Romans 6:17; Colossians 3:15
- faith: Mark 11:23; Romans 10:10; Hebrews 3:12

In order to receive Deep Relief Now, you need to understand these connections between the emotions and the belly...the belly and the heart...the heart and the human spirit. God wants to release the anointing of His Spirit in your life, flowing to bring deep healing for yourself and others.

The Location of Your Thoughts

Everyone seems to know where their thoughts are located. Whenever Dr. Jen and I speak to a group of people and ask them where they *think*, they *all* instantly point to their head. There's no confusion on that one.

Thoughts are formed in the brain by (1) recalling information stored in your memory and (2) processing information by applying knowledge to make decisions and solve problems.

The conscious mind is aware of only a fraction of brain activity at any given time. But your entire life story, every minute detail, is actually stored away in your non-conscious mind.

You have forgotten far more than you remember. Have you ever heard anyone say, "I saw my whole life pass before my eyes" during a crisis? Long-forgotten memories were retrieved and brought into conscious awareness.

It's important to realize that every thought has a corresponding emotion. Have you ever felt nostalgic when you smelled something connected with a pleasant childhood memory? Like freshly baked cookies or the evergreen smell of Christmas?

Memories are stored as feeling–thought combinations. That's why some memories still make you feel sad and others stir up happy feelings. The thoughts that cause us the most trouble, of course, are those connected to negative emotions.

The Location of Your Emotions

Most people associate the heart with emotions. That's why Valentine's Day **hearts** mean **love**.

Your *Bible heart* is the seat of the emotions,[1] the center of our inward life,[2] the hidden springs of our personality,[3] and the sphere of divine influence.[4]

According to scripture, then, your Bible heart is the *center of* emotion (Matthew 5:28, Luke 24:32, John 16:22, Ephesians 5:19), and your *Bible heart* is in the belly.

In modern terminology, we talk about gut hunches, gut feelings, or gut reactions. Often people are told to "go with their gut" when making decisions. This means it generally works out better to listen to the heart in addition to the head. Our choices are usually wiser when they're based on more than mental reasoning.

Think about it. Would you want to marry someone based solely on logical analysis? It's doubtful that either one of you would be very happy in the long run!

Emotions, the Gut, and Physical Health

As a child, did you ever "get butterflies in your tummy" when you anticipated a special holiday, prepared for the first day of school, or found out your grandparents were getting you a special gift? Likewise, you've probably known about children who get tummy aches when they're emotionally distraught. They feel their emotional pain in the belly.

Medical researchers and health professionals have known for a long time that physical health is connected to emotional health. Negative emotions are harmful to the physical body. And because the gastrointestinal tract is so closely linked with emotions, negative emotions commonly disrupt the digestive organs or even lead to eating disorders.

Women suffer from irritable bowel syndrome and functional somatic disorders at least twice as often as men. These disorders are closely linked with anxiety, stress and mood disorders, and they tend to weaken the immune system and increase inflammatory activity.[6, 7, 8, 9, 10]

But although eating disorders have commonly been considered a woman's complaint, new research has shown that more men struggle with eating disorders than previously believed. A recent Harvard study found that, out of 3,000 people suffering from bulimia and anorexia, 25% were male, and 40% of the men were binge eaters.[11]

The Gut Knows

Did you know that people have an emotional response if they tell a lie? That's what is actually measured indirectly by a polygraph (lie detector) test, as emotions trigger physiological responses in the body.

A polygraph measures involuntary responses in a person's body when he or she experiences the stress associated with deception. Through a combination of medical devices that monitor physiological changes, the examiner determines the normal level for that particular person. Then he checks for variations in heart rate, blood pressure, respiratory rate, and sweatiness of the fingers, compared to normal levels.

Because some people learn to control these key responses through biofeedback, researchers have discovered what may be the ideal lie detector test. It measures gut responses and appears to be unbeatable. According to an article in *New Scientist* magazine:

> Truth may be found in the [gut], at least where lie-detector tests are concerned. Pankaj Pasricha and colleagues at the Medical Branch of the University of Texas used an electrogastrogram to measure nerve activity in the stomachs of 16 volunteers when they were either lying or telling

the truth. The team found a significant increase in activity when the volunteers were lying but no increase when they were telling the truth. "The gut has a mind of its own," says Pasricha. "Its nervous system acts independently." The work was presented . . . at the annual scientific meeting [2005] of the American College of Gastroenterology.[12]

The Location of Your Will

The Bible says that the center of choice, volition, is in the heart. And we have already established that your *Bible heart* is in the *belly*! *Vine's Expository Dictionary* says the heart is also the seat of the conscience, intention, and will.[13] In the Old Testament, the Hebrew word for "reins" is sometimes used for the will. The literal translation for reins is kidneys, which locates the seat of volition in the gut.

> *I the LORD search the heart, I try the reins [kidneys], even to give every man according to his ways, and according to the fruit of his doings (Jeremiah 17:10 KJV).*

Did you know that your willpower creates your own stress? Willpower is the force of your own will trying to control yourself, other people, and the circumstances of life.

As soon as you feel tense or stressed, chemicals are released throughout your whole body, and your muscles contract. Whenever you face a perceived threat, your body reacts by going into the self-protection mode. You feel it first in the gut.

Pay attention the next time a minor inconvenience occurs, and you'll notice that your muscles tighten in the gut. Although you might not realize it, you can learn to catch yourself at this early stage and let it go. However, if you continue to stay stressed, your muscular tension is likely to increase and spread to your back, shoulders and neck.

PRACTICE: Here are some simple ways you can test out the "gut principle." Stand up and allow yourself to fall back a little, but stop yourself before you actually fall down. (You may want to stand with your back against a wall, or have someone stand behind you when you try this.) Where do you feel the "stop"? In the gut. You stopped yourself as an action of your will. Now close your eyes and think of an unpleasant person you know or a situation that stresses you out. Pay attention to what you sense in the gut when you think about it.

When you are suspicious about someone's motives, you close your heart to them. Your heart has said, "No, I will not be vulnerable to that person." Your will opens and shuts the door of your heart. (Remember the "open and shutting" principle we pointed out in 1 John 3:17?)

When you feel tension in your gut, it's a sign that your willpower has been engaged. However, when you pray and trust God's help, you open your heart to Him, and you automatically relax.

Have you ever noticed the back belt worn by workers who lift heavy objects in the workplace? It wraps around the midsection and low back to support their spine and lower body. During times of stress, reflexive abdominal bracing occurs (imagine bracing yourself before a punch in the gut), signaling the abdominal muscles to tighten, functioning just like an internal back belt.

When someone tells you to "let it go," you can do that by releasing it from the gut. If you notice that you are becoming tense when you have a deadline coming up at school or at work, relax and let God help.

But the secret is learning *how* to do it, and this all begins with knowing location, location, location. Your inner distress is located in your heart—your belly or gut—and that's where the relief must come. In the following chapters, you'll learn more about the practical steps for receiving Deep Relief, and receiving it quickly.

END NOTES

1 Strong, J. (1990). *Strong's Exhaustive Concordance of the Bible*. Hebrew and Chaldee Dictionary, *lêb*, 3820. Nashville, TN: Thomas Nelson Publishers, 58.

2 Vine, W.E. (1981). *Vine's Expository Dictionary of Old and New Testament Words*. United States: Fleming H. Revell Company, 297.

3 ibid

4 ibid

5 Goddard, E., Barth, K., & Lydiard, B. (2007). Disorders Which Frequently Overlap With Irritable Bowel Syndrome: Can a Shared Neurobiology Explain Their Frequent Association? *Primary Psychiatry, 14(4)*, 69-73.

6 Drossman, D., Camilleri, M., Mayer, E., & Whitehead, W. (2002). AGA technical review on irritable bowel syndrome." *Gastroenterology, 123(6)*, 2108-2131.

7 Longstreth, G., Thompson, W., Chey, W., Houghton, L., Mearin, F., & Spiller, R. (2006). Functional bowel disorders. *Gastroenterology, 130(5)*, 1480-1491. Erratum in: *Gastroenterology, 31(2)*, 688.

8 Palsson, O. & Whitehead, W. (2005). Comorbidity associated with irritable bowel syndrome. *Psychiatric Annals, 35(4)*, 320-324.

9 Chang, L. (2006). Neuroendocrine and neuroimmune markers in IBS, pathophysiology or epiphenomenon. *Gastroenterology, 130(2)*, 596-600.

10 Drossman, D. (2006). The functional gastrointestinal disorders and the Rome III process. *Gastroenterology, 130(5)*, 1377-1390.

11 Hudson, J., Hiripi, E., Pope, H.G., & Kessler, R.C. (2007). The Prevalence and Correlates of Eating Disorders in the National Comorbidity Survey Replication. *Biological Psychiatry, 61(3)*, 348-358.

12 Hutson, S. (2005). The stomach cannot lie. *New Scientist Magazine*, online edition, issue 2524, 05. Retrieved 6 January 2010 from http://www.newscientist.com/article/dn8238.

13 Vine, W.E. (1981). *Vine's Expository Dictionary of Old and New Testament Words*. United States: Fleming H. Revell Company, 297.

chapter NINE
LEARNING ANOTHER LANGUAGE

by Dr. Jen

BEFORE I MET DENNIS, my prayer life consisted mostly of talking to God and praying through prayer lists for the needs of other people or myself. I went to prayer meetings from time to time, and that seemed to be the way most people prayed. Sometimes I read books or took courses that included written prayers, and I prayed those prayers too.

I had taken a number of courses on Christian counseling, and often they provided lists of prayers for healing the heart. Despite my best efforts to follow their suggested formulas, my own heart received only minimal healing.

This lack of true relief was frustrating, and I could tell I wasn't the only one. I observed that most people who were wounded seemed to struggle for a long time with their emotional baggage, despite many hours of therapy or seminars. Their ongoing problems seemed to stem from an inability to forgive, even though they had *tried* to forgive for months or years. My counseling training even taught that forgiveness was a long process.

When Dennis started explaining the principles we call Deep Relief Now, it was like learning a whole new language. Although I considered myself well-versed in both the Bible and psychology, somehow I had missed some fundamental keys for true healing of the heart.

Understanding the Heart's Door

The first lesson Dennis taught me was how to connect, commune and communicate with God. Sounds simple enough, doesn't it? Yet I found that I'd been missing out on some revolutionary concepts.

Imagine hearing a car pull up to your house, and you see your least favorite person in the whole world heading down the walk to your front door. Oh, no!

So what do you do? You put up a wall. That's a typical response of the will to perceived danger. You are closing off your heart to protect yourself. It is a *defense* mechanism.

Whenever you get tense, your will is what tightens up. When you are stressed, your willpower has taken over, as you attempt to control yourself, other people or circumstances.

PRACTICE: Close your eyes and focus on your heart. Picture that person you don't want to encounter. Now pay attention to how it feels in your gut. Tense? Apprehensive? Angry? Like a wall? You certainly don't feel like flinging the door of your heart open to them, do you?

Now picture a person you love. Perhaps your child, grandchild or best friend. Does your heart "soften" and feel more open and positive? Take note of these different feelings.

The heart has a door that gives the Lord access to fill your God-shaped hole. Jesus says He stands at the DOOR of the heart and knocks, waiting for us to open to Him. So we can choose, as an act of our will, whether or not to open:

> Behold, **I STAND AT THE DOOR** and knock: if anyone hears my voice and **OPENS THE DOOR**, I will come in to him and dine with him, and he with Me (Revelation 3:20).

What I always had missed was that the same door we open for Jesus to come into our heart at salvation is *still* the door we must open for Him in our daily lives. It's like a "valve" that can open or shut off our spiritual connection with Him.

Jesus challenged the religious leaders of His day:

> You have your heads in your Bibles constantly because you think you'll find eternal life there. But you miss the forest for the trees. These Scriptures are all about me! And here I am, standing right before you, and you aren't willing to receive from me the life you say you want (John 5:39-40 MSG).

For all their religious studies and efforts to please God, these leaders had missed the point. As Jesus told them, they couldn't see the forest for the trees. Often, this could be said about us as well. We focus on the details but fail to grasp the big picture.

At the time of salvation, our spirit experiences a new birth, enabling us to connect with a heavenly realm that was inaccessible before. The Bible says in John 4:23-24 that God is a spiritual being, and those who worship (acknowledge and honor) Him must approach Him in spirit and truth (the reality of who He is, the genuine instead of a counterfeit). Because of this, our connection with our Heavenly Father must be made by our spirit rather than through our intellect.

Thinking about God is not the same as actually making a *connection* with Him. I love how The Message renders Jesus' words in John 4:23-24:

> *Your worship must engage your spirit in the pursuit of truth. That's the kind of people the Father is out looking for: those who are simply and honestly themselves before him in their worship. God is sheer being itself— Spirit. Those who worship him must do it out of their very being, their spirits, their true selves, in adoration.*

I encourage you to read this passage one more time, and let it really sink in. Ask God to make this kind of intimacy with Him a reality in your life.

Dropping Down

When Dennis and I sat down to pray, he told me to close my eyes and focus on God. He explained that when believers pray, they automatically make a spirit to spirit connection with God.

Dennis taught me to "drop down" to Christ in my heart. That simply meant I needed to get out of my head (my intellect) and make an inner connection with Christ in my heart (my spirit).

As believers, we have an inner pipeline directly to the fountain of living waters. However, when we don't focus on our spiritual relationship with the Lord, it's like closing up the line with a shutoff valve.

Instead of being just some kind of mystical theory, this has practical applications in our daily lives. For example, A member of our church testified to me that she could "drop down," commune with the Lord, and stay in peace even while she was having dental work done.

But often we have misconceptions that hinder our ability to apply the "drop down" principle. In my case, I had grown up believing I must pray to a God who was far, far away in heaven. Even though I knew I had invited Jesus to come into my heart, I still approached prayer as a long- distance call, which automatically created a feeling of separation. I later discovered that many others have the same misconception.

Yet the Bible says we can know God personally and intimately, as our Immanuel, or "God with us":

They shall call His name Immanuel, which is translated, "God with us" (Matthew 1:23).

Christ in you, the hope of glory (Colossians 1:27).

The kingdom of God is within you (Luke 17:21).

If you've given your heart to Christ, He isn't "way out there," but rather "right in there." Paul wrote about this vital truth in Romans 10:6-8:

*The righteousness of faith speaks in this way, "Do not say in your heart, 'Who will ascend into heaven?'" (that is, to bring Christ down from above) or, "'Who will descend into the abyss?'" (that is, to bring Christ up from the dead). But what does it say? "The word is **NEAR YOU**, in your mouth and **IN YOUR HEART**" (that is, the word of faith which we preach).*

The Bible says Christ will make His home in our hearts when we invite Him in. So there's no need for a long-distance call when you're talking with God. He is right there with you.

Christ will live in you as you open the door and invite him in (Ephesians 3:16 MSG).

The Peace of Connecting With God

Whenever I made a connection with the Lord in prayer, Dennis told me to pay attention to how it felt. I noticed that I instantly felt a sense of peace. However, if I opened my eyes and started thinking about house repairs or all the reports I had to write for work, my peace changed into mild anxiety. Yet as soon as I went back to prayer, the anxiety left and I felt the same peace again. My worries faded away.

I tried this exercise numerous times, and the result was always the same. When I focused on repairs or reports, the anxiety came back. But when I closed my eyes and made a prayer connection again, God's perfect peace returned!

This shouldn't really have surprised me, for it's exactly what the Scriptures promise:

You will keep in perfect peace all who trust in you, all whose thoughts are fixed on you! (Isaiah 26:3 NLT)

Don't worry about anything; instead, pray . . . Then you will experience God's peace, which exceeds any-thing we can understand. His peace will guard your hearts and minds as you live in Christ Jesus (Philippians 4:6-8 NLT).

Peace. Inner tranquility. Freedom from stress or fear. These verses say we can experience God's peace in any situation.

However, this must go beyond memory verses—it must become a personal discovery. What a joy it was to finally learn how to experience what God has promised in His Word all along. Every time I made a connection with Him in prayer, my internal conflict dissipated, and I felt deep peace inside.

> **PRACTICE:** Close your eyes and pray. Pay attention to Christ within, and be aware of how you feel inside. It will help you focus if you place your hand on your gut. Notice that there is a gentle perception of peace.

One of the biggest delights of a mother or father is hearing a child say, "Mama," or "Dada" for the very first time. Although a child is born with an ability to learn the language of his or her parents, the skill must be learned, and that takes time and practice.

In my early days as a Christian, I had little confidence in my ability to hear from God. Of course, I believed He still communicated with humankind. But when He spoke to me personally, I often questioned, "Was that really God, or did I just imagine it?" I was still a novice in how to hear and understand the language of the Spirit.

However, I gradually learned a principle that really helped me, and I know it will help you as well: Although God communicates to us in many different ways, His Love Nature is always attached to His voice. So no matter how He seems to be speaking to you, you can know it's truly Him if it's wrapped in love and faithful to His written Word.

The Language of Emotions

I learned from Dennis that the peace and joy I felt in prayer were manifestations of the love of God described in the fruit of the Spirit in Galatians 5:22-23: "The fruit of the Spirit is love, joy, peace, longsuffering, kindness, goodness, faithfulness, gentleness, self-control [temperance]."

Have you ever felt joy in your child's achievement, compassion when they suffered a disappointment, or tender affection as you gazed upon their sleeping face? It's all the same love, but it comes in different expressions depending on the situation.

In the natural realm, there are two broad categories of emotions. Human emotions are either love-based or fear-based. Everyone likes to feel the love-based emotions. If we could pick just one emotion, most people would choose to be happy all the time. People dislike negative, fear-based emotions so much that they spend a lot of time and effort trying to numb them through drugs, alcohol, or sex addictions.

Medical science has discovered that emotions play a major role in physical health. It is well documented that love-based emotions are good for the body, but fear-based emotions often lead to disease. Fear-based emotions not only are toxic, they're sometimes even deadly!

In describing the traumatic events of the end times, Jesus says one of the signs will be "men's hearts failing them from fear" (Luke 21:26). How amazing that people can literally be scared to death.

God's Emotions

In addition to love-based and fear-based emotions, the Bible says there's a third category of emotional experience available for believers: *God Emotions*. The God Emotions are even better than human love-based emotions. Since they spring from God Himself, the Bible calls these emotions *"the fruit of the Spirit"* (Galatians 5:22-23).

God is an emotional God! When we encounter the God who is Love, it shouldn't surprise us that our emotions are impacted in a positive way. God doesn't just *have* love, He **IS** Love!

We are made in God's image (Genesis 1:26-28). And just as we have human emotions, He has supernatural God Emotions. When we sense the love and presence of God, our emotions touch His emotions. As He touches our emotions with His love, we literally experience the love, joy, peace and hope of God:

> *May the God of hope fill you with all joy and peace*
> *as you trust in Him, so that you may overflow with hope*
> *by the power of the Holy Spirit (Romans 15:13 NIV).*

It's crucial to understand that this experience has nothing to do with human effort or a self-help program. When God's love is added into the mix, we experience *supernatural* love, joy, peace and the other types of fruit of the Spirit.

That's why Jesus says His peace is much deeper than anything the world can give us:

> *Peace I leave with you, My peace I give to you; not*
> *as the world gives do I give to you. Let not your heart be*
> *troubled, neither let it be afraid (John 14:27).*

God's peace is the peace "which surpasses all understanding," and it "will guard your hearts and minds through Christ Jesus" (Philippians 4:7). The word translated "understanding" here is the Greek word *nous*, which includes thoughts, choices and emotions. God's supernatural peace is supremely better, higher, and more excellent than anything that comes from our human thinking, choosing or feeling.

Hearing God's Voice

Have you ever questioned whether or not you're really able to hear from God? Jesus says four times in John 10 that His sheep can both hear and recognize His voice:

> *He who enters by the door is the shepherd of the sheep. To him the doorkeeper opens, and **the sheep hear his voice**; and he calls his own sheep by name and leads them out. And when he brings out his own sheep, he goes before them; and the sheep follow him, for **they know his voice.** Yet they will by no means follow a stranger, but will flee from him, for they do not know the voice of strangers . . . And other sheep I have . . . and **they will hear My voice** . . . **My sheep hear My voice,** and I know them, and they follow Me (John 10:2-5, 16, 27).*

Of course, it's possible to *hear* but not *understand*. A child hears parental voices even in the womb, but it takes a few years to understand everything that is said. The Bible tells us that sometimes people can hear God's voice, but not understand what He means. In John 12:28-30, God spoke from heaven and said, "I have both glorified [My name] and will glorify it again." The people who stood by could hear Him speak, but they just thought it had thundered!

God wants to speak to His people, and He wants them to understand His words. Look at some of the diverse ways He uses to speak to us:

1. The Bible (2 Timothy 3:16, Psalm 119:11, Psalm 119:105)
2. The still, small voice of the Holy Spirit (Acts 16:6-7, 1 Kings 19:12-14)
3. Creation and the world of nature (Romans 1:20)
4. The audible voice of God (Acts 9:4-5)
6. Dreams and visions (Matthew 1:20-21, Acts 10:9-18)
7. Angels (Luke 1:26-38, Acts 8:26)
8. Circumstances and apparent coincidences (Genesis 24:14-16)
9. Inner assurance and peace (Romans 8:16, Acts 27:10-13, 1 Colossians 3:15)
10. People (Acts 9:17)
11. Revelation and illumination (2 Corinthians 4:6, Ephesians 3:3, Galatians 1:12)
12. Our conscience (Romans 2:15)

Learning God's Love Language

Children are meant to learn the language of their parents in an atmosphere of a loving relationship. Likewise, when a person wants to have a close relationship with someone from a different culture, they make an effort to learn their language and customs. In fact, researchers have found that even adults, who have a more difficult time mastering unfamiliar languages than children, learn a new language more easily if they fall in love with someone who speaks that language.

One thing we know for sure is that "God is love" (1 John 4:9). Whenever He speaks, love is automatically attached to His words. In the same way, love is the motivation behind all of His actions. And when we respond back to Him in love, it creates a mutual relationship in which we can discover the love language of God.

Have you ever realized that you notice something more if it's important to you? For example, if you are interested in purchasing a certain make and model of car, you begin to see similar cars everywhere on the road, although you never paid attention to them before.

Dennis encouraged me to be aware of even gentle whispers of the Holy Spirit while in prayer. I began to notice that the presence of God felt stronger at certain times than others. I noticed that His presence seemed to decrease when I became distracted by a household chore or preoccupied with irrelevant thoughts. And when I read my Bible, I learned to linger over certain verses which were accompanied by an increased sense of God's presence in my life.

I was gaining a keener perception of subtle changes in the spiritual atmosphere. As my spiritual awareness became more finely tuned, it was like learning a whole new language. Instead of being merely an academic exercise, this new discernment was a critical ingredient in experiencing Deep Relief and passing it on to others as well.

chapter TEN
LORD, TEACH ME TO PRAY!

by Dr. Jen

MY PRAYER LIFE RADICALLY CHANGED as Dennis began teaching me to pray. I had been making the mistake of praying to God far away in heaven, but Dennis instructed me to focus on Christ within. Although I knew intellectually that I'd invited Jesus into my heart when I was saved, it was a new experience to learn what it means to open my heart and yield to Him moment by moment.

Dennis had developed keen discernment about God's presence, and he told me he could sense the Spirit's anointing as soon as I was in prayer. I learned to feel the difference, too, so I didn't have to just take his word for it.

Then Dennis gave me a helpful key for focusing on Christ within. He told me it would be easier to stay focused on my heart if I kept a hand on my belly. For a number of months, that suggestion really helped to keep my thoughts from wandering during prayer.

Let me be clear. This wasn't some kind of weird form of Eastern meditation. I didn't repeat any mantra or phrase over and over again, nor did I try to make my mind "blank." I simply became more aware of God and less distracted by my thoughts.

With Dennis' encouragement, I learned to linger in that place of prayer. I discovered that the more I yielded, the more God's presence increased. As I allowed Him to be in control, I was increasingly able to sense His nearness.

He must increase, but I must decrease (John 3:30).

PRACTICE: Try it yourself. Close your eyes in an attitude of prayer. Yield your heart to the Lord. How does it feel inside? That is having an "open" heart. Now open your eyes and think about unpleasant work situations or unfinished chores you have to do. How does *that* feel? Close your eyes and pray again. Pay attention to the difference.

Making the Heart Connection

One definition of prayer is *spiritual communion*. And another way to think of communion is "heart connection," which is necessary for any true relationship to occur.

Think about it. You cannot have a close relationship with someone unless you care. When you're truly involved with another person relationally, you genuinely care for them. Hearts become "knit together in love," as Paul describes in Colossians 2:2.

This "knitting" of hearts is why we use phrases like *"bond* of love," *"bonding* between mother and baby," or becoming *"attached* to someone." Communion implies connection. Paul speaks of this in Ephesians 4:3, when he says we should be "endeavoring to keep the unity of the Spirit in the bond of peace."

Love begins with emotional motivation accompanied by decision. The Bible says we have the ability to either open or shut the door to our hearts. When we are around another person, we either can open the door and connect with them, or we can shut the door and detach.

Becoming an Openhearted Person

Have you ever heard the term *openhearted*? This means being a person who is open emotionally. The door of our heart is open, and we are emotionally available to others.

Paul points out to the believers in Corinth that his heart is open to them: "O Corinthians! We have spoken openly to you, our heart is wide open" (2 Corinthians 6:11). But in return, he requested the same openness from them: "Open your hearts to us. We have wronged no one, we have corrupted no one, we have cheated no one" (2 Corinthians 7:2).

Likewise, John writes of the open heart Christians should have toward those in need: "Whoever has this world's goods, and sees his brother in need, and shuts up his heart from him, how does the love of God abide in him? (1 John 3:17).

As long as your heart is open to God, you are in prayer. If you are worried, stressed, angry or preoccupied with the cares of life, then you have disconnected from God at that moment. You've temporarily lost your intimate connection with Him and are trying to go it alone.

Dennis taught me the amazing simplicity of prayer. No complicated formulas are needed, for prayer is simply communing with God. I learned to enjoy just being with the Lord and perceiving His presence. I didn't follow any system, but simply wanted a real relationship with a real God. While I sometimes asked God for specific requests, my overwhelming passion was to know Him better.

Simple prayer was the first and primary revelation I received from God during my times with Dennis. As intimacy in prayer was birthed, I found my inner pain and feelings of rejection being miraculously healed. I was in the early stages of experiencing what we've come to know as Deep Relief Now.

A Passion to Know God

My times of prayer were not focused on "talking to God" but simply on experiencing His loving presence and enjoying fellowship with Him. I found that prayer didn't have to be a boring religious exercise or something just to cross off our daily To-Do List. Instead, it became the most exhilarating and enjoyable part of my life.

Later, I read several books on prayer, but by that time I only had one, all-consuming prayer request: to know Him more. The books about prayer were confusing to me at first, because they focused almost entirely on petitioning God with our prayer requests. I became convinced that the approach I was learning from Dennis was much more satisfying, and that realization settled the question for me.

The passion of my heart was expressed in this scripture verse from the apostle Paul:

> *[For my determined purpose is]* **that I may know Him** *[that I may progressively become more deeply and intimately acquainted with Him, perceiving and*

recognizing and understanding the wonders of His Person more strongly and more clearly] (Philippians 3:10 AMP).

I encourage you to stop for a minute, right now, and let these words sink deeply into your heart. Today can be the start of an exciting new beginning in your prayer life, enabling you to understand "the wonders of His Person more strongly and clearly."

chapter ELEVEN
LEARNING INTIMATE PRAYER
by Dennis

AFTER I HAD KNOWN THE LORD for about 14 years, I felt that I already had a deep prayer life. Yet I sensed the Lord prompting me to request with new determination, "Teach me to pray!" After this divinely initiated request, He began to lead me on a fantastic journey of inner transformation and greater intimacy with Him.

Over a period of six months, the Lord wooed me closer to Him through a step-by-step process of abiding in prayer (John 15:5). I was then able to begin teaching these same Spirit-directed steps to others, and I later compiled them into distinct areas, or levels, of Intimate Prayer.

> *I am the vine, you are the branches. He who abides in Me, and I in him, bears much fruit; for without Me you can do nothing (John 15:5).*

God taught me these levels in Intimate Prayer one at a time, staying on the same subject for several weeks or even months. Each step led me into greater intimacy and vulnerability in a loving, two-way relationship.

Every level of revelation about Intimate Prayer involved an inner work that allowed Him to search and purify my heart. As the Lord and I took this daily journey, He captured more and more of my heart, cleansing me of double-mindedness and impurity. I gained an acute awareness and sensitivity to His presence and the whisper of His Spirit.

This purification process wasn't always easy or pleasant, but it drew me closer and closer to the heart of God. I saw there was no other pathway to intimacy, for Jesus taught us, "Blessed are the *pure in heart*, for they shall *see God*" (Matthew 5:8).

Prayer Steps

Are you ready to embark on YOUR journey toward greater intimacy with God? You see, the key to experiencing Deep Relief Now is not a matter of psychological formulas, but rather intimacy with your Heavenly Father as a PERSON.

This begins with coming before the Lord with anticipation, expecting to meet with Him and experience His presence. As you draw near, present yourself to Him as a living sacrifice, ready to yield to His Spirit and His voice.

Remember that you are coming to honor and adore God. As you come boldly before the throne of grace (Hebrews 4:16), devote this time to seeking God for Himself alone. As you set out on your journey toward Intimate Prayer, this is not the time to petition for your own needs or intercede on behalf of others, although petitions and intercession are certainly important for a later stage.

As you enter more fully into His presence, allow God to show you any sins in your life. Receive His forgiveness and let Him wash and cleanse you with the water of His Word and renewing of the Holy Spirit (Titus 3:5). Don't condemn yourself, rather yield to God's love.

Don't be in a hurry! Be willing to linger at each stage in the process for as long as it takes to turn each relational principle into a deep and lasting inner work. As you learn each lesson in vulnerability, dependence and intimacy, He will teach you even more. But the attitude of your heart must be focused on the simplicity of pursuing a more intimate relationship with the Lord. This attitude of simplicity and humility is the good soil where the fruit of intimacy begins to grow.

Undivided Attention

As you come to present yourself to the Lord, there's an amazing fact you need to remember: He is giving you His undivided attention. Whether you realize it or not, you are His constant delight. Every time you draw close to Him, it ravishes His heart, because He loves you that much.

Understand that He is right there with you, as close as the very air you breathe. Think of this as the same way you would be aware of someone sitting in the back seat while you are driving a car. Although you can't always see the person, you know they are there.

Focus on the Lord, and allow His presence to flood your mind, will and emotions. As you do this, expect your surroundings to "slip away." Don't be surprised if you're so caught up with Him that you lose your sense of time.

In this process, you are likely to feel some initial resistance from your flesh. However, this will fade as you say "no" to distractions and stretch your capacity to remain in

His presence a little longer each time. Small victories will enable you to develop power to overcome flesh.

Four Touchstones to Remember

Intimate prayer is simple prayer. There are no complicated formulas to remember, nor any mantras to recite. As you progress in your journey, the principles will become second nature. You'll find yourself instinctively responding to the Lord, with no need for confusion or struggle.

But in the early phases of your journey in Intimate Prayer, there are four important perspectives to be aware of:

- **Honoring God as a Person.** As the Lord gives His full attention to you, you must acknowledge Him as a real Person who is present with you. You must come before Him in reverence (Hebrews 12:28), recognizing the great privilege it is to have in an audience with the King.

- **Listening to God.** *Listening* is *awareness* which includes the spiritual "inner knowings" of seeing, hearing, and touching. True listening means you gain an ever-increasing awareness and sensitivity to the Lord's presence and the promptings of His Spirit. This is a progressive lesson and is based on an unfolding discovery of who He is. You take the posture of a student before the Teacher, and you don't really have anything to say until you've first heard from Him (Isaiah 50:4).

- **Time spent with God.** Just as natural growth takes time, spiritual growth requires time as well. Part of the journey toward Intimate Prayer is learning to wait, and this is a necessary component in allowing God to heal and strengthen our heart: "Wait on the LORD; be of good courage, and He shall strengthen your heart" (Psalm 27:14). As you become accustomed to being with the Lord, you will be able to stay in prayer for longer and longer periods of time. Rather than being religious drudgery, this will be your joy and delight.

- **Function and flow.** The Gospels provide some powerful keys for how to function and flow in the Spirit, and we will cover these in depth in a later chapter. For now, just remember that God has given you the spiritual capacity to receive from Him and release His agape love to others.

Constant Communing

I found that praying once or twice a day was one thing, but experiencing constant communion with God was quite another. This kind of communion is about maintaining our spiritual connection with the Lord all day long. We don't see our prayer times as being like stops to a gas station to fill our car, for we are *continually* being filled with His presence.

Picture what it would be like to be married to someone, but to limit your time together to five or ten-minute spans, once or twice a day. What if you made your partner stand on the front porch the rest of the time, patiently waiting until you found a few minutes that were convenient for you to get together?

Who would tolerate a relationship like that? Yet, that's a pretty accurate picture of how many Christians treat their relationship with the Lord.

The Bible teaches God's design for marriage partners to be "one flesh" and describes the parallel with our spiritual intimacy with the Lord: "He who is joined to the Lord is ***one spirit with Him***" (1 Corinthians 6:16-17). Instead of being a sporadic on-again, off-again relationship, our communion with the Lord is meant to be 24 hours a day, 7 days a week, and 365 days a year.

"Dropping Down"

Often, our mind is one of the biggest barriers to the kind of spiritual communion I'm describing. When Jen and I first started praying together, I often reminded her to focus on Jesus rather than on her own thoughts. We coined the phrase *"drop down"* to describe the need to stop thinking and start praying. In other words, our focus had to drop from our head to our heart.

Early in our marriage, we were driving together to Home Depot, and Jen's mind was agitated with thoughts of new flooring tiles, hardware to replace a door knob, and similar concerns. Her mind raced with questions like, "Did I remember to bring the room dimensions? And "Should I put up some extra shelves and make a pantry out of that closet?" Her inner peace evaporated, and I remember telling her, "Jen, you need to drop down!"

Instantly, she could make the prayer connection again. Her thoughts stopped racing, and her inner peace returned. She again experienced what Paul wrote about to the Colossians: "Let the peace of God rule in your hearts" Colossians 3:15).

Communion Defined

I've found that many people come from church backgrounds where the concept of "communion" in prayer is a foreign concept. Others think I'm advocating some form of Eastern meditation, which is certainly not the case at all.

Communing is all about enjoying a mutual relationship with another person. It may be defined as *having an intimate relationship* or *sharing thoughts and feelings*. The Bible tells us that communion with the Lord and with other believers is meant to go beyond a mere intellectual or emotional relationship—it is also *spiritual fellowship*.

In John 15:1-5, Jesus tells us to *abide* in Him, which means staying connected with Him. He wants us to stay connected in spiritual fellowship with Him, and this means not just once in a while or every now and then. It means *all the time*.

In the early days of our relationship, I remember encouraging Jen to keep growing in her relationship of communion with God. "Include Jesus in your life moment by moment," I told her. "Pay attention to the difference you feel when you connect with Jesus, not only in your prayer times, but also throughout the day." Although this wasn't easy for her at first, it eventually became a way of life.

In the Gospels, we learn that Jesus sometimes chose to be alone for prayer for extended periods of time. However, Jesus was in fellowship with His Father *all* the time. He maintained a spiritual connection. Even amid jostling crowds in the noisy marketplace, Jesus was communing with Father God.

> *Then Jesus answered and said to them, "Most assuredly, I say to you, the Son can do nothing of Himself, but what He sees the Father do (John 5:19).*

"Whatever I say is just what the Father has told me to say" (John 12:50 NIV).

The apostle John gives us the wonderful news that *we* can have this same experience of communion with God. Of course, John enjoyed a very close relationship with Jesus during His time on earth. But the relationship didn't end there. John writes that he is *still* having fellowship with Christ, and we can too.

From the very first day, we were there, taking it all in—we heard it with our own ears, saw it with our own eyes, verified it with our own hands. The Word of Life [Jesus] appeared right before our eyes; we saw it happen! And now we're telling you in most sober prose that what we witnessed was, incredibly, this: The infinite Life of God Himself took shape before us. **We saw it, we heard it, and now we're telling you so you can experience it along with us, this experience of communion with the Father and His Son, Jesus Christ.** *Our motive for writing is simply this: We want you to enjoy this, too. Your joy will double our joy! (John 1:2-4 MSG).*

So if prayer is primarily about relationship, then we can stay in prayer as long as we maintain a connection, or communion. Even though you won't talk to God continuously, you *can* learn to stay plugged in.

This means it's truly possible to abide with Him and "pray without ceasing" (1 Thessalonians 5:17). But it all begins with a passionate quest to know Him better and ask, "Lord, teach me to pray" (Luke 11:1).

Intimate Prayer is a foundational ingredient for experiencing Deep Relief Now. Now you're ready for the next section of the book, on how healing prayer can quickly relieve your emotional pain.

— part six —
HEALING PRAYER

chapter **TWELVE**
WHAT MUST I DO TO BE SAVED?

——————— by Dr. Jen ———————

HAVE YOU EVER STRUGGLED in your Christian life? I sure did. Everything either seemed too hard, took too long, or simply didn't work.

I remember one preacher saying to take a piece of paper, write down a problem, then crumple it up and stomp on it. Well, I did what he said, but nothing changed in my life.

Once I tried to forgive someone. I not only *tried*, but I tried and tried and tried—yet I continued to hurt inside. I confessed forgiveness, cried about forgiveness, and even wrote and signed a forgiveness prayer in my journal. When none of those things relieved my distress, I sought prayer during altar calls, read countless books, and claimed every Bible promise that seemed to apply.

For some reason, true freedom was elusive. The festering sore in my heart wouldn't go away. What a mystery! I knew I must be missing something, but I couldn't figure out what it was.

When I met Dennis and began learning what the Lord had taught him about forgiveness, the answers were so

111

simple. How had I overlooked them for this long? I had believed well-meaning but erroneous church teachings and faulty paradigms of my own.

In order to experience true forgiveness and deep relief, I had to learn a brand-new perspective and think outside the box. It became a season of reeducation for me—a time to learn new things and unlearn old things. Everything Dennis taught me was extraordinarily simple, yet so profound.

This new approach to Christian living was stated in a nutshell by the apostle Paul: "So then, just as you received Christ Jesus as Lord, continue to live in Him" (Colossians 2:6 NIV). Simply put, as believers we must *continue* living in Christ in the *same way* we received Him at our initial salvation.

Do you remember how you got saved? Well, Paul says the key to living the Christian life was given to us at the very first moment of our salvation. Let me explain…

Belief and the Emotional Heart

In contrast with the head, what characteristics do you associate with the word HEART? The physical heart pumps our blood, and this action is necessary to keep the body supplied with oxygen and nourishment. But scripture tells us that our spiritual heart supplies us with spiritual life, or zoë:

> *For God so loved the world, that he gave his only begotten Son, that whosoever believeth in him should not perish, but have everlasting LIFE [zoë] (John 3:16 KJV).*

The Bible says we must *believe* in our hearts (Romans 10:9-10) to connect with God's zoë life, and the heart is EMOTIONAL. That means that *salvation* must include emotions. Love, Valentine's Day, broken hearts, open-hearted—all of these have to do with our emotions, relationships or romantic life. You cannot have a real relationship that doesn't include the emotions.

> *As the Father loved Me, I also have loved you; abide in My love (John 15:9).*

> *Beloved, let us love one another, for love is of God; and everyone who loves is born of God and knows God. He who does not love does not know God, for God is love (1 John 4:7-8).*

Sometimes the head and the heart can be in conflict. If our thinking is twisted by carnal reasoning, it can cause us to ignore an important "gut hunch" the Lord wants us to pay attention to. On the other hand, if our emotions are dominated by our flesh, they can lead us to make bad decisions. So it's very possible to think, speak or do one thing, while your heart is saying just the opposite.

> *[Jesus] answered and said to them, "Well did Isaiah prophesy of you hypocrites, as it is written: This people honors Me with their **lips**, but their **HEART** is far from Me (Mark 7:6).*

Opening Your Heart's Door

When you were saved did you ask Jesus into your HEAD...or into your HEART? Most people laugh when you ask that. Believers seem to intuitively understand that they welcomed Jesus into their hearts. Why is this important? Because *belief* in Jesus is relational, or *emotional*. Real relationship always involves making an *emotional* connection. You must open your heart to *care* about a person.

Paul explains it this way:

*If you acknowledge and confess with your lips that Jesus is Lord and in your **heart believe** (adhere to, trust in, and rely on the truth) that God raised Him from the dead, you will be saved. [10]For with the **heart** a person **believes** (adheres to, trusts in, and relies on Christ) and so is justified (declared righteous, acceptable to God), and with the mouth he confesses (declares openly and speaks out freely his faith) and confirms [his] salvation (Romans 10:9-10 AMP).*

There is an emotional DOOR in your heart. That is what the term openhearted means—there's a door in your heart which you can open or shut. When you open that door to God, you make a heaven connection.

Behold, I stand at the DOOR and knock. If anyone hears My voice and OPENS THE DOOR, I will come in to him (Revelation 3:20).

The Bible says you must believe in your heart in order to be saved. This how you entered into God's Kingdom and the Christian life: you believed and opened your heart.

It's not enough to agree with the Bible in a philosophical way. Believing that Jesus was a good man and that His teachings are admirable is mental assent—not saving faith. You must welcome Him as your Lord and Savior.

The Other Steps of Salvation

If you can open something, you can also close it. When you open the door in your heart to God, you instantly make a heaven connection and are no longer separated from the Lord. However, if you close the door, intentionally or inadvertently, you cut off your fellowship with Him.

In addition to OPENING your heart, there are two other notable parts of your initial salvation experience: You asked Jesus for FORGIVENESS and you experienced PEACE with God. This was not just earthly peace, but the supernatural peace that "surpasses all understanding" (Philippians 4:7).

Just as these three words—open, forgiveness and peace—were key characteristics of your conversion experience, they are likewise the keys to walking in a victorious life in Him.

Remember Paul's words:

*So then, **just as you received Christ** Jesus as Lord, continue to live in Him (Colossians 2:6 NIV).*

As you have therefore received Christ . . . walk (regulate your lives and conduct yourselves) in union with and conformity to Him (Colossians 2:6 AMP).

So, if we're supposed to *live in Christ* in the same way as we *received Him initially*, what does that mean? How did we receive Christ when we were first saved?

The steps in salvation, simplified, are:

1. **Open.** You opened the door of your heart and invited Jesus to come in.

2. **Forgiveness.** You acknowledged that you were a sinner, received forgiveness, and were cleansed of your sins.

3. **Peace.** You instantly experienced an amazing and supernatural sense of peace: "Therefore, having

been justified by faith, we have peace with God through our Lord Jesus Christ (Romans 5:1).

Let's take a deeper look at how these steps apply to our ongoing relationship with the Lord...

Peace With God

When you *opened* the door of your heart to Jesus, you became emotionally available to Him. Then you received His gift of *forgiveness* and experienced *peace* with God.

In order to open your heart to Jesus, you had to let down your guard and allow yourself to trust Him. This meant becoming vulnerable.

Why do we put up walls in the first place? To protect our hearts so we won't be hurt. Walls are an inner resistance based in fear and suspicion.

When Dennis and I started praying together, I realized I sensed a deep peace whenever I was in prayer. I could get anxious about home repairs, but as soon as I prayed and gave it all to God, the anxiety quickly changed to peace.

Remember: Peace is not just an absence of external conflict. Even if two countries are not engaging in active warfare, when the inhabitants have hostility toward each other, they are not truly at peace. Likewise, if two people are courteous in public but are belligerent deep in their hearts, they certainly are not at peace. Their words and gestures may hide their internal war, but they are at war nonetheless.

In a practical sense, peace is an emotion. It is experienced as an absence of inner turmoil and the presence of deep calmness. Paul describes this as one of the first signs of our salvation:

Therefore, since we are justified (acquitted, declared righteous, and given a right standing with God) through faith, let us [grasp the fact that we] have [the peace of reconciliation to hold and to enjoy] peace with God through our Lord Jesus Christ (the Messiah, the Anointed One) (Romans 5:1 AMP).

So, if this incredible peace is a mark of our initial salvation, what does it take to maintain our peace as a part of our moment-by-moment relationship with the Lord? One of the clues is to recognize that peace is one of the "God Emotions" available as a fruit of the Holy Spirit.

Fruit of the Spirit

I remember Sunday school lessons on the fruit of the Spirit when I was a child, but this was always a mystery to me. Often we were told that the fruit required a choice to submit our lives to God, but we shouldn't expect to *feel* anything.

Once I went to a women's conference on joy, yet nobody there seemed to *have* any joy or know how to get it. This seemed very strange to me. I understood the principle of accepting God's blessings by *faith*, but shouldn't we *experience* something too?!

When I got saved, I was thrilled with Jesus and the new life He had given me. I know this was more than just a mental concept for me. I was truly different inside, and everyone told me how much I had changed. Something brand new had happened in my heart, and I felt much more secure and peaceful. I overflowed with all kinds of good emotions, just as Paul prayed the Christians in Rome would experience:

> *I pray that God, the source of hope, will **fill you completely with joy and peace** because you trust in him. Then you will **overflow with confident hope** through the power of the Holy Spirit (Romans 15:13 NLT).*

You see, God *Himself* experiences emotions. He's not just a stoic, emotionless cosmic force—He FEELS love, anger and pain. That's why the Bible speaks of both "the JOY of the Lord" (Nehemiah 8:10) and "the WRATH of God" (Romans 1:18).

Likewise, we see Jesus' emotions when He stood before the tomb of His friend Lazarus and was surrounded by the grieving siblings, Mary and Martha: "Jesus wept" (John 11:35). And we see His anger when He removed the moneychangers from the temple (John 2:14-17). Even after Jesus' death, resurrection and ascension, we see Him as a high priest who is "touched with the feeling of our infirmities" (Hebrews 4:15 KJV).

In many ways, "the fruit of the Spirit" Paul describes in Galatians 5:22-23 are "God Emotions"—the emotions the Holy Spirit wants to replicate in the lives of God's people.

God transforms our entire being through the process of sanctification. Sanctification is the ongoing practical experience of being set apart for God's work and being molded into the image of Christ.

In Romans 12:2 the Bible tells us that transformation occurs through the renewing of the mind. However, the word Paul uses for "mind" is *nous* in the Greek. This refers to thoughts, will and *emotions*. Our thinking is changed by revelation from God, our will yields to God's will, and our carnal emotions are transformed by the fruit of the Spirit.

And do not be conformed to this world, but be transformed by the renewing of your mind [thoughts, will, and emotions], that you may prove what is that good and acceptable and perfect will of God (Romans 12:2).

A Gateway to Knowing God

While it's no doubt true that people are sometimes deceived and led astray by *unsanctified* emotions, it's also true that God wants to *redeem* our emotions. He wants our emotions to resonate with the God Emotions of His Spirit.

Jonathan Edwards (1703-1758) was a preacher, theologian, missionary to Native Americans, and the father of the First Great Awakening in America (1730-1760). Contrary to the views of many people of his day, Edwards said the emotions are the gateway to knowing God. He added that he doubted the reality of a person's salvation unless their emotions were deeply impacted.

Why are many believers today so reluctant to allow the Lord to work through their emotions? Jesus didn't preach a merely cerebral faith, but rather told His disciples they should expect to *experience* His peace: "Peace I leave with you, My peace I give to you; not as the world gives do I give to you. Let not your heart be troubled, neither let it be afraid" (John 14:27).

While writing to the Philippians from a jail cell, Paul used the words *joy* or *rejoice* 18 times in only 104 verses. In addition to telling the believers in Philippi to rejoice always, he exhorted them to be content and free from anxiety:

> *Rejoice in the Lord always. Again I will say, rejoice! . . . Be anxious for nothing, but in everything by prayer and supplication, with thanksgiving, let your requests be made known to God; and the peace of God, which surpasses all understanding, will guard your hearts and minds through Christ Jesus (Philippians 4:4, 6).*

Paul is describing a special kind of peace, available through an intimate, abiding relationship with Christ. This amazing, supernatural peace, Paul said, is better than our rational understanding, and it will guard and protect our "hearts and minds" (Philippians 4:7).

God loves us so much that He doesn't want us to live in fear or torment. He sent His Son to come and rescue us from the kingdom of fear and bring us into the Kingdom of Love. Even while we were still sinners, Jesus came to die for us and set us free.

> *[God] has delivered us from the power of darkness and conveyed us into the kingdom of the Son of His love (Colossians 1:13).*

> *You did not receive the spirit of bondage again to fear, but you received the Spirit of adoption by whom we cry out, "Abba, Father" (Romans 8:15).*

> *Inasmuch then as the children have partaken of flesh and blood, He Himself likewise shared in the same, that through death He might destroy him who had the power of death, that is, the devil, and release those who through fear of death were all their lifetime subject to bondage (Hebrews 2:14-15).*

The encouraging message of these verses is clear: *You don't have to live in fear or torment!*

The Fruit of Love

The love described in 1 Corinthians 13 is love springing from the very heart of our Father God. Every manifestation of the fruit of the Spirit (Galatians 5:22-23) is just a different expression of God's love:

> *But the fruit of the Spirit is love, joy, peace, longsuffering, gentleness, goodness, faith, meekness, temperance: against such there is no law (Galatians 5:22-23 KJV).*

Picture pure white light shining through a prism. As the prism separates the white light into a spectrum of colors, the colors of the rainbow are revealed. After passing through the prism, it's the same white light, but the different wavelengths contained within it are made visible.

Jesus refers to Himself as "the light of the world" (John 8:12). The Bible describes a rainbow—multicolored rays of light—surrounding the throne room in heaven (Revelation 4:3). The pure light of His presence is refracted into all the colors of the rainbow, and more.

In a similar way, God's love is refracted into all the various forms of the fruit of the Spirit. No wonder Paul says "love is the fulfillment of the law" (Romans 13:10). If we walk in God's love, all of His other commandments are kept.

God's Love for YOU

For many people, God's love is merely a doctrine or a memory verse. They can recite John 3:16 about God so loving the world, but this has never become their personal experience.

What about *you*? Have you opened the door of your heart to the Lord—not just at your salvation, but also in your daily relationship with Him since then?

God's longing heart for relationship is revealed in the parable of the prodigal son (Luke 15:11-32 NIV). The father grieved when his son was gone, and he rejoiced when his son came to his senses and returned home. However, through it all, the father loved his son and yearned for a close relationship with him.

What an emotional God! The father was watching so intently that he saw his son even while he was quite a distance away from home. Filled with love and joy, he forgot both decorum and age as he ran to greet and embrace his child: "While he was still a long way off, his father saw him and was filled with compassion for him; he ran to his son, threw his arms around him and kissed him" (v. 20).

God is waiting for you to draw even one step nearer to Him, and He will have compassion and run toward you. He wants you to be at peace with Him, experiencing a peace that surpasses your understanding.

> *I am leaving peace with you, I give My peace to you:*
> *I am giving to you, not just as the world would give.*
> *Your heart must not ever trouble you and it must stop*
> *being timid (John 14:27 PNT).*

But perhaps you're not like the younger son in this story—you might be more like his older brother. Both sons were estranged from their father, but we don't see that until the end of the story, when the older son refuses to enter the father's house and celebrate his brother's return: "The older brother became angry and *refused to go in*" (v. 28). How sad! The older brother allowed an offense to keep him from OPENING THE DOOR and participating in the party.

As wonderful as it is to be saved, God *also* wants us to experience the JOY of our salvation (Psalm 51:12). He wants us to "have and *enjoy life*, and have it in *abundance*" (John 10:10 AMP).

What must you do to be saved—and then live an abundant life *after* you are saved? God has already made provision for everything you need. All you need to do is open, receive forgiveness, and experience His peace!

How Do You Walk in the Spirit?

1. **OPEN.** Open the door of your heart and include Jesus in the moment.

2. **FORGIVENESS.** If you feel a negative emotion, forgiveness will instantly wash it out.

3. **PEACE.** As soon as you forgive, you experience peace again.

Forgiveness is the Key

Notice that "forgive" is the step between open and peace. If you don't know how to apply forgiveness in daily life, then a walk in the spirit will be mysterious.

chapter THIRTEEN
CHRIST THE FORGIVER

by Dr. Jen

IT'S IMPORTANT FOR YOU to understand that the principles of Deep Relief Now are not just some nice theory—they really *work*. Countless lives have already been transformed...and you can be next!

We've included some DRN success stories in the Appendix, but here are a few samples in the meantime.

INSTANT RECOVERY FROM BETRAYAL

After a trusted friend betrayed him, Rob lived with a continual undercurrent of resentment in his heart. Every time he thought about the other person, he got angry. Time and time again, Rob had said, "I forgive him"— but he remained a captive to his anger nevertheless. No matter how hard he tried, he couldn't shake his inner torment.

When Rob met with us, Dennis taught him how to use the How-To tools. In just a few short minutes, years of frustration and anger were replaced by deep peace. The constant emotional gnawing in his gut vanished and, as a bonus, he was instantly healed of irritable bowel syndrome (IBS)!

A RAPE VICTIM FINDS RELIEF

Candice could hardly remember life without inner pain. Since childhood, it had been her cruel daily tormentor. More than 50 years before, when she was a young child living in Germany, she had been raped by Nazi soldiers. Her mother had warned her to stay away from them, but she had been disobedient. And the guilt of disobeying her mother only compounded her deep feelings of shame.

We prayed with Candice, and her agony was gone in under five minutes!

Blown away by the rapid and complete relief from anguish and self-incrimination, Candice exclaimed, "That was too easy!"

Yet her pain was completely gone—and gone *permanently*. The following day she told us she felt like a brand-new person, clean and whole. Incredulous, she said, "After being tormented my entire life, now I am free!"

Rob and Candice both found Deep Relief, and they found it quickly and permanently. In both cases, forgiveness was one of the keys that set them free from their prison of torment.

Misconceptions About Forgiveness

If you've spent any significant time around churches, you've no doubt heard a lot about forgiveness. Yet why is this so difficult and confusing for most of us? We "try" to forgive, "choose" to forgive, and even "pray" to have strength to forgive—yet our unforgiveness and bitterness often remains.

One problem is that there are many misconceptions about forgiveness, and here are three of the most common ones:

- **"If you forgive someone, it lets them off the hook for the harm they've done."** No, the perpetrator must still answer to God after you forgive them, and sometimes they must also suffer legal penalties for their actions.

- **"If you forgive someone, you must allow them back into your life."** No, even though God holds you responsible to forgive those who have wronged you, you still must use wisdom and maintain appropriate boundaries.

- **"Forgiveness is necessary for the *big* emotional traumas, but it's not required for small offenses."** No, even small fears, offenses and hurt feelings can fester and cause ongoing emotional, relational and physical harm if not dealt with properly.

Before we continue, take a few moments to pray and ask the Lord to show you if you've unwittingly adopted any of these misguided views about forgiveness. Ask Him to show you the truth about how this has negatively impacted your life.

Christ the Forgiver

Christ is the Forgiver. Jesus forgave us, He gave us the gift of forgiveness, and we forgive others by His grace which works in us. Christ the Forgiver does all the work!

> *I, even I, am He who blots out your transgressions for My own sake; And I will not remember your sins. (Isaiah 43:25).*

In Him we have redemption through His blood, the forgiveness of sins, according to the riches of His grace (Ephesians 1:7).

Even as Christ forgave you, so you also must do (Colossians 3:13).

You must right now forgive our sins for us, in the same manner as we have completed forgiving everyone of everything, big and little, against us (Matthew 6:12 PNT).

Now take a look at what forgiveness IS and IS NOT:

Forgiveness IS NOT:

- *Not* releasing someone from their responsibility
- *Not* being a doormat
- *Not* removing the consequences of someone's actions
- *Not* absolving someone's sin
- *Not* pretending to forget
- *Not* unconditionally reconciling with a person when boundaries still need to be established

Forgiveness IS:

- Forgiveness comes from a Person. Christ is the Forgiver, and He wants to do His forgiving work through us.

- Forgiveness is a heart matter, and it must include the mind, will and emotions in order to be complete.

- Forgiveness releases the person doing the forgiving, freeing them from the poison of toxic emotions.

- Forgiveness releases perpetrators so that God can work in their lives.

- Forgiveness cancels the debt held against the other person.

- Forgiveness is ceasing to sit in the place of judgment.

- Forgiveness is commanded by the Word of God. It is not optional.

Again, take a few minutes to meditate on these principles, asking God to apply them to your life through His Spirit.

Real World, Practical Forgiveness

You would be surprised to learn how many Christians—that's right, *Christians*—are offended at the suggestion that they might need to forgive. "I've already done that!" they adamantly claim. However, their forgiveness has never yet dealt with their emotions or the deep issues of their heart.

Most Christians sincerely want to get the "forgiveness thing" right. Their religious pride is hurt if you suggest they still may be trapped in a prison of anger and unforgiveness. In many cases, they probably just need a better explanation of forgiveness.

Many believers don't understand how practical forgiveness is for everyday life. We don't have to wonder whether or not we've truly forgiven someone who has wronged us, for there are telltale symptoms your unforgiveness remains:

- Do you still feel hurt inside because of what someone did to you in the past?

- Are you still angry when you talk about some injustice that was done to you?

- Do you still cringe when you think of someone—perhaps a family member, coworker, church member or pastor?

- Do you find yourself going out of your way to avoid someone, even though they've asked for your forgiveness and you have no reason to fear them?

If you answered yes to one or more of these questions, it doesn't mean you haven't *tried* to forgive the other person. It just means your emotions have not yet been impacted. Only then can you truly be free emotionally.

What does this mean? It means you need to experience *complete* forgiveness, not just *trying to* forgive. Forgiveness is a supernatural experience, exchanging negative emotions for peace. That's the only thing that will deal with your emotions and bring relief once and for all.

A husband and wife scheduled a prayer appointment with us a few years ago. They came in and sat down on the sofa, and we asked them to close their eyes and pray. When we asked the wife to tell us where she needed to apply forgiveness, she smiled and said, "Oh, I have forgiven *everyone* in my whole life!"

Immediately, her husband looked at her in astonishment and said, "Well, what about your sister Eleanor and our neighbor Karl? And what about your anger toward our son Andy for not coming home for Thanksgiving? And don't forget being mad at your mother for always criticizing your cooking and...."

Stories like this are more common than you can imagine. Many people are simply out of touch with their emotions and what's really going on in their heart. Psychologists like to call it *denial*, and that's part of it. However, it's also a self-induced numbness that causes us to tune out our unpleasant emotions. That doesn't mean they've gone away—we've simply stuffed them deep into non-conscious memory where they are buried alive.

What about you? If you feel an unpleasant emotion when you think of any person or situation, then you still need some real world, hands-on forgiveness.

The truth is that *none* of us has fully dealt with every single unresolved hurt, offense or fear we've encountered in our entire lifetime. You would have to be *perfect* in order to accomplish that feat. And if you actually believe you are perfect, you have an even *bigger* problem than you realize—and you need forgiveness for trying to be God!

chapter FOURTEEN
EASY DOES IT
by Dr. Jen

FORGIVENESS DOESN'T NEED to be complicated or difficult. Yet Dennis and I have made a startling discovery as we've ministered in numerous churches and Bible schools, with hundreds of prayer appointments with individuals seeking relief from their inner pain. Shocking as it may sound, we have noticed that between 90-99% of the Christians we minister to have no idea how to forgive effectively enough to deal with their negative emotions.

Occasionally, someone will forgive another person "accidentally," even though they don't know what they did or how they did it. One example of this is that of Corrie Ten Boom. During the Nazi occupation of Holland in WWII, Corrie and her sister, Betsie, were sent to Ravensbruck concentration camp after they were caught hiding Jews in their home.

After the war ended, Corrie was giving her testimony in a church in Munich. Following her stirring message about the forgiveness of God, a man made his way through the crowd to speak to Corrie. She was aghast when she realized he had been one of the guards at Ravensbruck, but he did not recognize Corrie as a former inmate. He told her he had been a guard at a concentration camp during the war, but had since been forgiven by God. Now he was a fellow Christian. Smiling broadly, he stretched out his hand to shake Corrie's hand.

And I, who had spoken so glibly of forgiveness, fumbled in my pocketbook rather than take that hand. He would not remember me, of course—how could he remember one prisoner among those thousands of women?

But I remembered him and the leather crop swinging from his belt. I was face-to-face with one of my captors and my blood seemed to freeze...It could not have been many seconds that he stood there—hand held out—but to me it seemed hours as I wrestled with the most difficult thing I had ever had to do.

For I had to do it—I knew that...

And still I stood there with the coldness clutching my heart. But forgiveness is not an emotion—I knew that too. Forgiveness is an act of the will, and the will can function regardless of the temperature of the heart. '... Help!' I prayed silently. 'I can lift my hand. I can do that much. You supply the feeling.'

And so woodenly, mechanically, I thrust my hand into the one stretched out to me. And as I did, an incredible thing took place. The current started in my shoulder, raced down my arm, sprang into our joined hands. And then this healing warmth seemed to flood my whole being, bringing tears to my eyes.

'I forgive you, brother!' I cried. 'With all my heart!'[1]

I wonder how many people tried to forgive by shaking hands after reading Corrie's story.

It wasn't shaking hands but the God encounter that accomplished the forgiveness. As she obediently reached her hand out to the guard, she forgave by the grace of Christ the Forgiver in her heart.

A man named Charlie told us that he had forgiven when he pretended a pillow was the neck of a perpetrator. He strangled the pillow, then somehow the anger left as he let go. Charlie accidentally forgave, or let go, in his heart as he let go with his hands. We explained to Charlie that forgiveness didn't take place in his hands, his heart cooperated with Christ the Forgiver.

Much quality ministry has happened to us at times even though we didn't understand how it happened or how to make it happen again.

If you don't know how to do something properly, you may just keep doing the wrong thing repeatedly hoping that it might work. Occasionally the heart cooperates with the words or actions, but forgiveness is not in shaking hands, letting go of an object, or praying long enough and hard enough. That is why some have adopted the theory that forgiveness is a process. Many have genuinely tried to forgive but they have tried the wrong way.

A few years ago, we invited a young French woman to stay with us for several weeks. She had lived in France her whole life and had never visited America before. When we arrived home from the airport, we showed her where everything was in the rooms where she would be staying. Then we spent a short time talking and said our good nights.

In the morning, we were dismayed to discover she had been awake until 2 a.m. trying to figure out how to turn off the lamps in the bedroom. Finally, she gave up and just unplugged the lamps so she could get some sleep. Apparently American lamps have different switches than French lamps! We showed her how to turn the switches on and off. It was easy when she knew how.

Forgiveness is the same way. When you know how to do it the right way, it's easy. We've seen people who struggled with this for years "turn the forgiveness switch" in mere moments after they learned the secret.

Forgiveness Sets YOU Free

Jesus said bitterness and resentment are like jailers that keep you imprisoned (Matthew 18:21-35). The person who did you wrong may be living a happy, carefree life, but your own feelings take *you* captive. You replay the situation repeatedly in your head, and you feel a churning in your gut every time you think about them.

What you may not know is that even the cells of your body are being poisoned by your anger. It's like you gulping down a vile cup of poison, while saying smugly, "I'll show *them!*"

The following story from the news in San Diego is a dramatic testimony of forgiveness in the face of horrendous circumstances:

Molly LaRue's body was found next to her dead fiancé. They were murdered by serial killer

Paul David Crews in September 1990 while hiking on the Appalachian Trail.

Sixteen years later, just before Christmas, Molly's father, Jim LaRue, was in a Pennsylvania courtroom reading a one-page letter of forgiveness to Crews when his death sentence was commuted to life in prison without parole.

"Most people think you are forgiving the perpetrator and they're off scot-free and you get nothing," says LaRue, who lives in a suburb near Cleveland. "It's just the opposite. When you forgive a person, you're deciding to be freed."

He has no doubt that forgiveness has been good for him. "I have the energy to focus on other things," he says. Before, "there were always nagging, gnawing thoughts in the background. You pay a price for that."[2]

Forgiveness washes away buried pain and brings healing for even the deepest emotional traumas. It replaces toxic emotions with the peace of God. However, you don't have to reserve it for times of enormous injury. Forgiveness is also freely available to cleanse every bit of guilt, embarrassment, anger, bitterness, anxiety, regret, fear, hate and grief—whether large or small.

Forgiveness has internal cleansing power. We experience this cleansing for the first time at conversion, when the sin barriers that separated us from God are washed away.

Think about that for a moment. You opened your heart, experienced forgiveness and cleansing, and were no longer separated from God (1 John 1:9). With the barriers removed, you instantly experienced peace.

But forgiveness is not meant to be a one-time, or a just-when-I-really-need-it, gift that we keep on the shelf the rest of the time. Jesus also gave us the gift of forgiveness for *everyday use*. You can hang it by the bed as you sleep and take hold of it when your feet hit the floor in the morning.

Unforgiveness Makes You Sick

Medical doctors and researchers have found clear evidence that physical health is closely connected to emotional health. For a long time, researchers have realized that emotional baggage often leads to disease.

Some researchers make a distinction between stress and emotions. But stress is fear-based, so it is emotional too.[3]

Since the 1990s, scientific research has been exploding on the subject of forgiveness. Research indicates a strong correlation between unforgiveness and sickness.[4] Medical doctors and researchers are turning to forgiveness as one of the primary keys for dealing with toxic emotions.

This is quite a dramatic reversal of scientific opinion. Scientists and medical doctors used to scoff at the idea that "unquantifiable emotions" could be given any consideration in serious medicine. However, the results of extensive research cannot be denied.

Emotions release a flood of chemical reactions into the body, and these directly influence every organ at the cellular level. In time, your emotions are written into your cellular memory. Over a lifetime, your *biography* becomes your *biology*. Your brain is in constant dialogue with your gut and your entire body through the emotions. Your mind and body are not just connected—they are unified in one system. This mind-body unity is now undisputed by researchers.

Although negative emotions don't *directly* cause disease, they create the conditions by which diseases can develop. There is actually a new field of medicine called psychoneuroimmunology, or psychoneuroimmunoendocrinology, which treats the toxic interactions between emotions and physiology.

Emotions and Physical Health

Although there is merit in our culture's current emphasis on exercise and nutrition, it doesn't matter much what else you do if you are poisoning your body with negative emotions. It should come as no surprise to learn that Dennis and I see many physical healings occur when a person forgives. Here are just a few samples:

'THE REJECTION AND THE CANCER DISAPPEARED!'

"First, I got healed of rejection from my mother. After that, I was amazed to see a skin cancer on my arm get smaller and smaller over the next few weeks, until it totally disappeared. My doctor was simply astounded. I didn't have to have surgery! It was just gone!" —J.L., Charlotte, North Carolina

"MY ARTHRITIS IS GONE!'

"I was so twisted up with arthritis that I could barely use my hands. I could hardly bear the pain at times. But when I prayed with the Clarks and received emotional healing, my arthritis went away too. My fingers have straightened out and, praise God, there's no more pain!" —R.M., Mt. Pleasant, South Carolina

Anger and hostility may even lead to early death. A long-term study showed that people who score in the high range on hostility scales are almost five times more likely to die of heart disease than those scoring lower. Furthermore, they were seven times more likely to die by age 50.[5]

Chronic pain has been linked to toxic emotions. Dr. John Sarno, professor of rehabilitative medicine in New York University School of Medicine, found that 88% of his patients had a wide range of negative emotional issues which were affecting them physically. When he treated the underlying emotions, he observed that his patients rapidly improved, and many were permanently cured.[6]

Stress, Aging and Fear

Stress is a combination of emotional distress and physical tension. It arises from a fear-based negative perception of one's ability to control the circumstances of life.

Toxic emotions can lead to stress even when our circumstances don't warrant it. Buried emotions cause internal pressure. The exertion of willpower, which is necessary for emotional suppression, generates stress regardless of our external situation. In other words, we can actually create our own stress.

The emotional toll of chronic stress accelerates the normal aging process in the body. A study published by

Elissa Eppel in 2004 documents how chronic stress speeds up the aging process on a cellular level. Stress alters the immune system and our ability to produce blood cells. It is also associated with physical frailty, osteoporosis, inflammatory arthritis, cardiovascular disease, and general functional decline.[7]

About 40 million American adults age 18 years and older suffer from anxiety disorders. That is approximately 18% of the population in a given year.[7] Anxiety disorders are the most common form of mental illness in the United States. Anxiety disorders include panic disorder, obsessive-compulsive disorder (OCD), post-traumatic stress disorder (PTSD), generalized anxiety disorder (GAD), and phobias (social phobia, agoraphobia, and specific phobia). [8, 9, 10, 11]

Many diseases have been linked with fear and anxiety, [12] including skin disorders such as eczema and psoriasis, high blood pressure, cardiovascular diseases, digestive conditions such as ulcers, colitis, irritable bowel syndrome (IBS), and Crohn's disease.

A month or two after Dennis and I were married in 1997, I was jerked awake out of a sound sleep by a rapidly racing and pounding heartbeat and a cold sweat. I knew exactly what was happening: paroxysmal atrial tachycardia (PAT). This consists of extremely rapid heartbeats for a period that begins and ends abruptly. The heart rate suddenly shoots upward to 140 to 220 beats a minute, and it feels like it simply won't slow down.

My heart was beating so fast that it felt like the bed was shaking. This was not a new thing, but a symptom that had tormented me several times a month for the last 20 years. Dennis awakened and felt my fear flooding the room.

Fortunately, he helped me pray through this, and I felt the fear leave instantly. My heart immediately stopped palpitating and returned to a gentle, normal rhythm. The atrial tachycardia never recurred!

Remember: Heart health—like so many other aspects of our physical body—is linked to toxic emotions, including fear, stress, depression and anger.[13, 14]

Shame, Depression and Repressed Emotions

Guilt and shame are often associated with depression. Guilt arises from a sense of having done something wrong. Shame usually arises from a perception of personal unworthiness, embarrassment, disgrace or dishonor.

A person suffering from guilt or shame typically reflects it in their body language, such as lowering their gaze to avoid eye contact, hanging their head down, or walking with drooping shoulders. Often, such a person feels helpless and hopeless, and these feelings can lead to social isolation and depression.

Depression has been linked to heart disease,[15] osteoporosis,[16] and cancer.[17]

It's important to understand that you can't find deep relief from your emotional pain by merely suppressing your negative emotions. Suppressed negative emotions don't actually go away, they're just hidden away under the surface of your conscious awareness.[18] Emotions don't die. We just "bury them alive."

Suppressed emotions function much like termites, secretly eating away at the wooden structure of a house.

Although the homeowner might not even realize termites are there, the destruction continues.

The suppression of negative emotions adversely affects the cardiovascular system.[19] Emotional suppression is also associated with an increase in coronary heart disease[20] and cancer.[21, 22, 23]

Consider the words of Gabor Maté, MD, a Vancouver physician and the author of *When the Body Says No: The Cost of Hidden Stress*[24]:

> "I never get angry," says a character in one of Woody Allen's movies, "I grow a tumor instead." In over two decades of family medicine, including seven years of palliative care work, I have been struck by how consistently the lives of people with chronic illness are characterized by emotional shutdown: the paralysis of "negative" emotions—in particular, anger.

> This pattern holds true in a wide range of diseases from cancer, rheumatoid arthritis and multiple sclerosis to inflammatory bowel disorder, chronic fatigue syndrome, and amyotrophic lateral sclerosis (ALS) . . .

> The suppression of anger contributes to the onset of cancer and other diseases because the mind and body cannot be separated. The brain's emotional centres are directly and powerfully linked with the immune centres throughout the body. Emotions such as anger serve exactly the same defensive role as the immune system: to protect our boundaries and to keep us from being overwhelmed by external forces. Similarly, both emotions and the immune system, when healthy, also serve a repair function: they help us to heal

when we have sustained some trauma or when something has gone wrong internally.[25]

The Science of Forgiveness

Scientific research on forgiveness has exploded since the 1990s, and hundreds of studies by researchers in many fields are focusing on everything from the emotional, mental and physical benefits of forgiveness to the relational and societal implications. The social sciences have linked forgiveness to social bonding in communities, overcoming the effects of violent crimes, improved physical health, and having successful marriages.

Forgiveness is literally good for your heart. A study in the *Journal of Behavioral Medicine* links forgiveness with lower blood pressure and also with stress relief.[26] Another study correlates forgiveness with needing less medication and experiencing better quality of sleep, less fatigue, alleviation of various physical symptoms, and an improvement in overall physical health.[27]

An article published in the January 2008 issue of the Mayo Clinic *Women's HealthSource* states that, "Holding a grudge appears to affect the cardiovascular and nervous systems. In one study, people who focused on a personal grudge had elevated blood pressure and heart rates, as well as increased muscle tension and feelings of being less in control. When asked to imagine forgiving the person who had hurt them, the participants said they felt more positive and relaxed and thus, the changes dissipated. Other studies have shown that forgiveness has beneficial effects on psychological health, too."[28]

Dennis and I regularly see people experience dramatic physical healings as a result of forgiving others. A young mother had been diagnosed with four serious medical conditions. A friend gave her our materials, which explained how forgiveness and the God Tools for emotional health also impact physical healing. When she prayed through her painful memories and toxic emotions, her symptoms disappeared. A new round of medical tests verified that she was completely healed.

The Gift of Forgiveness

We should pay very close attention to someone's dying words. Consider this story…

In the final days before Angela's husband died, he tried to tell her all the important things she would need to know after his passing. She strained to hear every word and wrote down everything he said.

The dying husband told Angela how much he loved her, of course. But he also told her details about important practical matters, such as which people she could trust with financial matters, what to do, and what to avoid. She kept a meticulous record of all these things. Everything he told her proved to be crucial for the future life she led. How grateful she was for his love and guidance!

In the same way, Jesus chose His final words carefully before He died on the cross. Forgiveness was so important for our redemption that Jesus declared it through His final prayer for mankind and His final action on behalf of one man. First, He prayed, "Father, forgive them" (Luke 23:34). Then He forgave a criminal hanging on the cross beside Him: "Assuredly, I say to you, today you will be with Me in Paradise" (Luke 23:43).

Jesus died to give you this wonderful gift of forgiveness. All Christians recognize that this gift of forgiveness was the key to their initial salvation and right standing with God. There is no substitute for forgiveness. It is the indispensable gateway to God's Kingdom.

However, as vital as forgiveness is for our initial entrance into the Christian life, it is so much more than that. Forgiveness is *also* our key to the elusive "abundant life" that Christians talk about but too rarely experience.

A Process or Instantaneous?

When you first received Christ, you opened your heart to Him, received forgiveness, and instantly experienced peace. This is wonderful, but Paul goes on to say we should "so walk" in Christ, in the same way we received Him:

> As you have therefore received Christ . . . [so] walk (regulate your lives and conduct yourselves) in union with and conformity to Him (Colossians 2:6 AMP).

The word "walk" refers to the way you live everyday life. This is the way to make forgiveness a lifestyle instead of a one-time event.

Many experts have taught that forgiveness is a *process* that may take a long time. But think about this. Was your initial conversion a process, or was it instantaneous? As soon as you asked Him to come in, Jesus was there for you. When you first received forgiveness from Him, did you have to fast, plead or experience a long delay? Of course not. When you got saved, you didn't have to work for forgiveness or beg God for it, you just received it by opening the door of your heart in faith.

Forgiveness is not just a choice. It is a gift. Because of what Jesus did for us on the cross, forgiveness is freely available and easily accessible. It is the way to live life well. Forgiveness begins with a choice, but it ends with an encounter with Christ the Forgiver.

Experiencing Christ the Forgiver

Before I met Dennis, I tried and tried to forgive. To my surprise, Dennis told me that had been the whole problem: I was *trying* to do it. He pointed out that it's by grace through faith that we are saved (Ephesians 2:8-9). Grace is the personal presence of Christ empowering us to be all that He has called us to be and do all that He has called us to do.

The Apostle Paul wrote that "It is no longer I who live but Christ who lives in me" (Galatians 2:20-21) which suggests that it is also no longer I who loves, nor I who forgives. Christ is He who forgives through us. We do not extend forgiveness by ourselves, from ourselves. Forgiveness is a Person, an encounter with Someone, a supernatural exchange.

Christ the Forgiver living inside me does all the work. True forgiveness requires encountering Christ the Forgiver, rather than merely knowing and reciting scripture verses, or merely a *doctrine* of forgiveness.

It is no longer I who love, but Christ who loves in me. It is no longer I who forgives but Christ the Forgiver who forgives through me. And that's not just true of the mighty apostle, it's true of every believer. It is the power of Christ Himself in us and working through us: "Christ in **you**, the hope of glory" (Colossians 1:27).

So why do so many believers live in defeat and despair? Since Christ lives in them, the *potential* for victory is certainly there, but somehow they're failing to cooperate with that potential and appropriate that power.

Paul didn't just see this in some kind of abstract theoretical or theological way. No, it was a *reality* to him. He actually allowed Christ to live through him, and he realized that was the secret of the Christian life.

Unfortunately, it's entirely possible to go on living as we lived before, in the power of our own flesh and intellect. Rather than letting Jesus live His life through us, we can live a life of striving and struggle as we *try* to please God.

If you're like most of us, you've experienced this yourself. There have been times when you tried to live the Christian life in your own strength, or you tried to forgive someone in your own strength. In Romans 7, Paul described his own miserable experience with this misguided approach to the Christian life: "O wretched man that I am! Who will deliver me from this body of death?" (Romans 7:24).

So what is the answer? Look at this story from the life of Jesus:

> *[Jesus] entered Capernaum after some days, and . . . . many gathered together, so that there was no longer room to receive them, not even near the door . . . Then they came to Him, bringing a paralytic who was carried by four men. And when they could not come near Him because of the crowd, they uncovered the roof where He was. So when they had broken through, they let down the bed on which the paralytic was lying.*
>
> *When Jesus saw their faith, He said to the paralytic, "Son, your sins are forgiven you." And some of the scribes were sitting there and reasoning in their hearts, "Why does this Man speak blasphemies like this? Who can forgive sins but God alone?"*

But immediately, when Jesus perceived in His spirit that they reasoned thus within themselves, He said to them, "Why do you reason about these things in your hearts? Which is easier, to say to the paralytic, 'Your sins are forgiven you,' or to say, 'Arise, take up your bed and walk'? But that you may know that the Son of Man has power on earth to forgive sins"—He said to the paralytic, "I say to you, arise, take up your bed, and go to your house."

Immediately he arose, took up the bed, and went out in the presence of them all, so that all were amazed and glorified God, saying, "We never saw anything like this!" (Mark 2:1-12).

The scribes were upset that Jesus told the paralytic that his sins were forgiven. Why? They reasoned correctly that only God can forgive sins. So by saying this, Jesus was making Himself the equivalent of God. Then He told them it was just as easy for Him to forgive sins as it was to heal a man who was paralyzed. Easy. Instantaneous.

Don't miss this point: Jesus said it was easy for Him to forgive sins! Of course, anything Jesus does is easy for Him, for He does "all things well" (Mark 7:37).

We make forgiveness hard when we try to do what only God can do. So what is the answer? Let the One who forgives sins do it! You somehow managed to cooperate with Him when you were born again. Was that hard? No. You simply yielded your heart and received forgiveness from Christ the Forgiver.

So remember Paul's words in Colossians 2:6 (NIV): "Just as you received Christ Jesus as Lord, continue to live in Him." Forgiveness isn't hard or complicated. Easy does it!

END NOTES

[1] Ten Boom, Corrie ((1971). *The Hiding Place*. Old Tappan, NJ: Chosen Books, Fleming H. Revel Co. 215.

[2] Dolbee, S. (2008). The healing power of forgiveness: Science measures physical as well as mental benefits. *San Diego Times Tribune*, August 16, 2008.

[3] Cannon, W. (1936). The role of emotion in disease. *Annals of Internal Medicine, Philadelphia, 9*, 453-1465.

[4] Worthington, E.L., Jr., Berry, J.W., & Parrott, L. III (2001). Unforgiveness, forgiveness, religion, and health. In T.G. Plante & A.C. Sherman (Eds.), *Faith and health: Psychological Perspectives*, New York: Guilford Press, 107-138.

[5] Barefoot, J.C., Dahlstrom, G., & Williams, R.B. (1983). Hostility, CHD incidence, and total mortality: a 25-year follow-up study of 255 physicians. *Psychosomatic Medicine, 45*, 59–63.

[6] Sarno, J. (1999). *The Mindbody Prescription: Healing the Body, Healing the Pain*. New York, NY: Warner Books. xviii-xxviii.

[7] Epel, E.S., Blackburn, E.H., Lin, J., Dhabhar, F.S., Adler, N.E., Morrow, J.D., & Cawthon, R.M. (2004). Accelerated telomere shortening in response to life stress. *Proceedings of the National Academies of Science, 101(49)*, 17312-17315.

[8] U.S. Census Bureau Population Estimates by Demographic Characteristics. Table 2: Annual Estimates of the Population by Selected Age Groups and Sex for the United States: April 1, 2000 to July 1, 2004 (NC-EST2004-02) Source: Population Division, U.S. Census Bureau Release Date: June 9, 2005.

[9] Kessler, R., Berglund, P., Demler, O., Jin, R., & Walters, E. (2005). Lifetime prevalence and age-of-onset distributions of DSM-IV disorders in the National Comorbidity Survey Replication (NCS-R). *Archives of General Psychiatry, 62(6)*, 593-602.

[10] Kessler, R., Chiu, W., Demler, O., & Walters, E. (2005). Prevalence, severity, and comorbidity of twelve-month DSM-IV disorders in the National Comorbidity Survey Replication (NCS-R). *Archives of General Psychiatry, 62(6)*, 617-27.

[11] Kessler, R., Berglund, P., Demler, O., Jin, R, & Walters, E. (2005). Lifetime prevalence and age-of-onset distributions of DSM-IV disorders in the National Comorbidity Survey Replication (NCS-R). *Archives of General Psychiatry, 62(6)*, 593-602.

[12] Cohen, S., Janicki-Devert, D., & Miller, G.E. (2007). Psychological Stress and Disease. *Journal of the American Medical Association, 298(14)*, 1685-1687.

[13] Brotman, D., Golden, S., Wittstein, I. (2007). The cardiovascular toll of stress. *Lancet*, 2007 Dec 1; 370(9602). 1828.

[14] Kubzansky, L. and Thurston, R. (2001). Emotional vitality and incident coronary heart disease: Benefits of healthy psychological functioning. *Archives of General Psychiatry*, 2007 Dec; 64. 1393.

[15] Rutledge, T., Reis, S.E., Olson, M., et al (2001). Psychosocial Variables Are Associated with Atherosclerosis Risk Factors Among Women with Chest Pain: the WISE [Women's Ischemia Syndrome Evaluation] Study. *Psychosomatic Medicine, 6*, 282-288.

[16] Yirmiyah, R., and Bab, I. (2009). Major Depression Is a Risk Factor for Low Bone Mineral Density: A Meta-Analysis. *Biological Psychiatry, Volume 66, Issue 5*, 1 September 2009, 423-432.

[17] Pyter, L., Pineros, V., Galang, J., McClintock, M., & Prendergast, B. (2008). Peripheral tumors induce depressive-like behaviors and cytokine production and alter hypothalamic-pituitary-adrenal axis regulation. *Proceedings of the National Academy of Sciences, 106 (22)*: 9069-9074.

[18] Gross, J. (1998). "The emerging field of emotion regulation: An integrative review." *Review of General Psychology, 2*, 271-299.

[19] Gross, J., & Levenson, R. (1997). Hiding feelings: The acute effects of inhibiting positive and negative emotions. *Journal of Abnormal Psychology, 106*, 95-103.

[20] Pennebaker, J. (1992). Inhibition as the linchpin of health. In H.S. Friedman (Ed.), Hostility, coping, and health. *Washington, DC: American Psychological Association*, 127-139.

[21] Gross, J. (1989). Emotional expression in cancer onset and progression. *Social Science in Medicine, 28*, 1239-1248.

[22] Jensen, M. (1987). Psychobiological factors predicting the course of breast cancer. *Journal of Personality, 55*, 317-342.

[23] Temoshok, L. (1987). Personality, coping style, emotion, and cancer: Towards an integrative model. *Cancer Surveys, 6*, 545-567. [24] Maté, G. (2003). *When the Body Says No: The Cost of Hidden Stress*. Canada: Knopf.

[25] Maté, G. (April 2004). Suppressing Our Emotions Harms Physical and Mental Health. Retrieved January 13, 2010 from Alive.com. April 2004. http://www.alive.com/1787a5a2. php?subject_bread_cramb=78.

[26] Lawler K., Younger J., Piferi R., Billington E, Jobe R, Edmondson K, & Jones W.H. (2003). A change of heart: cardiovascular correlates of forgiveness in response to interpersonal conflict. *Journal of Behavioral Medicine, 26*, 373-393.

[27] Lawler K., Younger J., Piferi R., Jobe R., Edmondson K., & Jones W. (2005). The unique effects of forgiveness on health: an exploration of pathways. *Journal of Behavioral Medicine, 28*, 157-167.

[28] Mayo Clinic (2008). Learning to Forgive May Improve Well-Being. (Wednesday, January 2, 2008), *Mayo Clinic Women's HealthSource*. Retrieved October 12, 2010 from the Mayo Clinic website: http://www.mayoclinic.org/news2008-mchi/4405.html

chapter FIFTEEN
THE GOD TOOLS
by Dr. Jen

SCRIPTURE TELLS US that we've *already been given* the God Tools for deep emotional healing, but few believers seem to know how to use them properly. Paul writes:

> *We use our powerful **GOD-TOOLS** for smashing warped philosophies, tearing down barriers erected against the truth of God, fitting every loose thought and emotion and impulse into the structure of life shaped by Christ (2 Corinthians 10:3-5 MSG).*

> *God is strong, and he wants you strong. So take everything the Master has set out for you, **well-made weapons** of the best materials. And **put them to use**... (Ephesians 6:10-11 MSG).*

Reality TV shows are popular these days, but the Christian experience should be the greatest reality makeover show of all time. But have you ever tried to keep New Year's resolutions? Or change a destructive habit? Or stop thinking certain thoughts?

The Bible talks about transformation, but many Christians don't seem to actually *experience* much transformation other than their initial salvation experience. What's the problem here? Paul explains:

> *PUT OFF . . . the old man . . . and . . . PUT ON the new man which was created according to God, in true righteousness and holiness (Ephesians 4:22-24).*

There is a *process* in between "putting off the old" and "putting on the new." How do you put off the old? How do you put on the new? If you don't understand how to do that process, there is little change.

In all my years of church experience before I met Dennis, I honestly couldn't detect much transformation in the lives of believers in my church or through Christian counseling ministries. In fact, I was getting very discouraged about the lack of spiritual progress I saw in most people, including myself.

I remember a time when my church was planning an evangelistic crusade. But as I looked around at the church members, I couldn't help thinking, "Maybe we should *first* do something to bring healing and victory to the believers we already have, before trying to make more converts like them!" It was so sad. Our church was filled with well-meaning Christians who were stressed out, wounded, grouchy, fearful and depressed. "What is wrong here? Shouldn't *Christians* be in better shape than this?" I asked myself.

Something That Works

I don't know about you, but I simply don't have time for theories or practices that don't work. None of us has time or energy to go on rabbit trails that become dead ends. We want biblical tools that bring true transformation.

Well, the good news is that the God Tools really work, and they can be applied easily to your life. I've been thrilled to discover both physiological and spiritual principles for transformation. And through Dennis' mentoring, I've learned why the God Tools work so well, and I've learned how to use them.

This is not a method, but a descriptive explanation that demystifies how to live in the spirit. If God is always present to save, then He is always present to sanctify. From the initial encounter with Christ to the subsequent relationship that follows we have documented a step-by-step practical explanation that combines God-encounter with process.

Let's take another look at Romans 12:2: "Do not be conformed to this world, but be transformed by the renewing of your **MIND** that you may prove what is that good and acceptable and perfect will of God."

The Greek word Paul uses for "mind" (*nous*) doesn't mean just your thoughts or what is going on in your head. *Nous* means your entire being, including your thoughts, will, emotions, reflective consciousness, perception and understanding. Your mind encompasses your whole heart, not just your thinking. And this includes your emotions.

The ramifications of this are huge. If a person truly wants to be transformed, something has to be done about their pesky emotions, not just their thoughts or intellectual questions. But of course, some people assume it's impossible to do much to change our emotions. They are *so* wrong! Our emotions—and the rest of our mind as well—can be transformed through basic, essential God Tools every believer has been given by the Lord. *You've already received all the spiritual equipment you need!*

God Tool #1: Prayer

Prayer is the first great God Tool. Here are the four main components of Simple Prayer listed again:

1. Honoring God as a Person
2. Listening to God (*listening* is *awareness* which includes the spiritual "inner knowings" of seeing, hearing, and touching)
3. Time spent with God
4. Function and flow

The first three elements were covered in Chapter 11, but now let's focus on the fourth element, ***function and flow***.

Jesus lived His life on earth in the function and flow of the Spirit. The early church followed Christ's example, cooperating with the moving of the Holy Spirit through loving intercession, releasing, receiving and forgiving.

Let's look at some specific examples.

Jesus was in constant communion with Father God, following His guidance as to what He was to do and say (John 5:19). This spiritual communion with the Father was of the utmost importance to Jesus:

> *I do nothing of Myself; but as My Father taught Me, I speak these things. And He who sent Me is with Me. The Father has not left Me alone, for I always do those things that please Him"* (John 8:28-29).

> *My food is to do the will of Him who sent Me, and to finish His work (John 4:34).*

When Jesus ministered in some way, He was aware of the "spiritual flow" that took place. When the woman with a hemorrhage was healed by touching the hem of

His garment, Jesus explained, "Someone did touch Me; for I perceived that [healing] power has gone forth from Me" (Luke 8:46 AMP).

Jesus encouraged His disciples that they could count on the Father to be with them too, giving them the right words to speak in every situation:

> *When they deliver you up, do not worry about how or what you should speak. For it will be given to you in that hour what you should speak; for it is not you who speak, but the Spirit of your Father who speaks in you (Matthew 10:18-20).*

The apostle John reminded his readers that he had experienced an incredibly close relationship with Jesus during His earthly ministry: "That which was from the beginning, which we have heard, which we have seen with our eyes, which we have looked upon, and our hands have handled, concerning the Word of life..." (1 John 1:1). But the story doesn't stop there. John went on to say that he was *still* experiencing Jesus' reality, many years after He ascended. And he said this same kind of relationship with the Lord was available to every other Christian as well:

> *. . . the life was manifested, and we have seen, and bear witness, and declare to you that eternal life which was with the Father and was manifested to us—that which we have seen and heard we declare to you, that you also may have fellowship with us; and truly our fellowship is with the Father and with His Son Jesus Christ. And these things we write to you that your joy may be full (1 John 1:2-4).*

How would you like your peace and joy to "be full"? That can be your experience today! It comes through having intimate, unhindered fellowship with Christ.

The Many Facets of Prayer

Like a beautiful diamond, prayer is a wondrous, many-faceted relationship with God. This includes loving intercession, releasing, receiving, forgiving, and resisting. Each of these facets is critical for experiencing and imparting the Deep Relief available in the presence of the Lord:

- **Loving intercession.** Jesus bridged the gap between heaven and earth. His intercession on behalf of mankind released heavenly power into the earthly realm. And He taught us to pray He would manifest more of the reality of His Kingdom "on earth as it is in heaven" (Matthew 6:10). Through our loving intercession, we can literally release heavenly rivers on earth:

  Whoever drinks of the water that I shall give him will never thirst. But the water that I shall give him will become in him a fountain of water springing up into everlasting life (John 4:14).

  He that believeth on me, as the scripture hath said, out of his belly shall flow rivers of living water (John 7:38 KJV).

  There is tangible spiritual substance in the prayers of believers. In the book of Revelation we're told that the prayers you release from your spirit are actually stored in heaven until it's time for them to be poured out and answered on earth:

  *Now when He [the Lamb] had taken the scroll, the four living creatures and the twenty-four elders fell down before the Lamb, each having a harp, and **golden bowls full of incense, which are the prayers of the saints** (Revelation 5:8).*

*Then another angel, having a golden censer, came and stood at the altar. He was given much incense, that he should offer it with **the prayers of all the saints** upon the golden altar which was before the throne. And the smoke of the incense, with **the prayers of the saints**, ascended before God from the angel's hand. Then the angel took the censer, filled it with fire from the altar, and **threw it to the earth**. And there were noises, thunderings, lightnings, and an earthquake (Revelation 8:3-5).*

PRACTICE: Close your eyes and "drop down." From your heart, yield to Christ within and allow loving intercession to flow out to your loved ones or friends. That is true intercession, "loving even without words."

- **Releasing (letting go).** Jesus said He came to earth to do the will of Father God rather than fulfill His own will. This means He released, or let go of, His own preferences and choices: "He knelt down and prayed, saying, 'Father, if it is Your will, take this cup away from Me; nevertheless not My will, but Yours, be done'" (Luke 22:41-42).

In the same way, believers are called to be obedient to God's will, making Jesus the Lord of their lives. This is not optional, but mandatory, if we are to live a victorious Christian life. Jesus once asked, "Why do you call Me 'Lord, Lord,' and not do the things which I say?" (Luke 6:46). Making Him Lord means yielding, releasing, letting go, and obeying what He tells us to do.

> **PRACTICE:** Close your eyes in prayer and "drop down," focusing on Christ in your heart. Can you picture any area of your life that causes you to feel tense? From your belly, yield and release it to God. As you release, let it go from your heart—not just mentally. Notice that you feel deep peace when you actually do release your painful or stressful areas to the Lord.

- **Receiving.** Jesus received a powerful spiritual baptism from His Father:

Jesus also was baptized; and while He prayed, the heaven was opened. And the Holy Spirit descended in bodily form like a dove upon Him, and a voice came from heaven which said, "You are My beloved Son; in You I am well pleased" (Luke 3:21-22).

On several occasions, the believers in the book of Acts received a similar spiritual impartation:

When the Day of Pentecost had fully come, they were all with one accord in one place. And suddenly there came a sound from heaven, as of a rushing mighty wind, and it filled the whole house where they were sitting. Then there appeared to them divided tongues, as of fire, and one sat upon each of them. And they were all filled with the Holy Spirit... (Acts 2:1-4).

When they had prayed, the place where they were assembled together was shaken; and they were all filled with the Holy Spirit, and they spoke the word of God with boldness (Acts 4:32).

This matter of "receiving" is found throughout the New Testament. In the book of Ephesians, Paul prays for believers to receive inner revelation and strengthening:

Therefore I also, after I heard of your faith in the Lord Jesus and your love for all the saints, do not cease to give thanks for you, making mention of you in my prayers: **that the God of our Lord Jesus Christ, the Father of glory, may give to you the spirit of wisdom and revelation in the knowledge of Him, the eyes of your understanding being enlightened;** *that you may know what is the hope of His calling, what are the riches of the glory of His inheritance in the saints, and what is* **the exceeding greatness of His power toward us who believe,** *according to the working of His mighty power (Ephesians 1:15-19).*

I bow my knees to the Father of our Lord Jesus Christ . . . **that He would grant you, according to the riches of His glory, to be strengthened with might through His Spirit in the inner man** *(Ephesians 3:14, 16).*

PRACTICE: Close your eyes in prayer and drop down. Yield to Christ within. Think of a favorite scripture verse. We are told that Christ is the Living Word. Yield to and receive the life of that verse in your heart. The goal is to hold your heart open until you meet the Author of the Word and encounter His mighty presence.

- **Forgiving.** Jesus not only forgave us, but He also instructed us to freely forgive others:

Peter came to Him and said, "Lord, how often shall my brother sin against me, and I forgive him? Up to seven times?" Jesus said to him, "I do not say to you, up to seven times, but up to seventy times seven" (Matthew 18:21-22).

The apostles, likewise, admonished believers to be forgivers: "Be kind to one another, tenderhearted, forgiving one another, even as God in Christ forgave you" (Ephesians 4:3).

- **Resisting.** Resisting is your God Tool that allows you to resist the enemy and hold your spiritual ground. It is a product of your spirit, not willpower. When you resist, you perceive the outside pressure, but feel the peace of God in your heart. Refuse to give in to the pressure. The enemy can't touch the fruit of the spirit.

Therefore, put on every piece of God's armor so you will be able to resist the enemy in the time of evil. Then after the battle you will still be standing firm (Ephesians 6:13 NLT).

God Tool #2: Forgiveness

Forgiveness is not only one of the facets of prayer, but it is also the second great God Tool. In the next chapter, we will get some practice in forgiving, but it's important to lay a proper foundation here first.

In an earlier chapter, we explained the scriptural location of your heart. God created you with a *door* in your heart that enables you to make a connection with Him in the Spirit. Now let's consider how connecting with God and encountering His forgiveness all works physiologically.

It's important to recognize that the brain is virtually unlimited in its potential for processing information. It can form vast numbers of connections, and there are practically no bounds on the amount of information it can process at any given time. However, you are totally unaware of 99.999% of what is going on inside your non-conscious mind.

So dealing with someone's thoughts and memories is like dealing with one grain of sand compared to all the sand on the beach. Years ago, I discovered that taking long case histories is usually a waste of time. You can get lots of information but still know nothing about how it's all connected.

That's why after years of talking, a therapist often still has no clue about what's really going on inside a client's head. Can you imagine sitting down and trying to chart out every little thing you do, every emotional reaction and ridiculous thought, trying to figure out where they all come from? And that is barely skimming the *surface*.

So what is *really* going on inside you? What things are tying you up in knots? What emotional roots are influencing your thoughts and actions? And how are all these things connected?

The point is you'll never be able to totally figure yourself out! Even the best counselors, therapists or psychiatrists would never be able to really figure you out. They can only guess. As Paul said, "We know in part and we prophesy in part" (1 Corinthians 13:9). And when it comes to understanding what's going on in the mind, we only know a *small* part.

But God doesn't guess. He knows exactly what the problem is, what caused it, and how to fix it. Look at the contrast between His complete understanding and our minuscule understanding:

We don't yet see things clearly. We're squinting in a fog, peering through a mist. But it won't be long before the weather clears and the sun shines bright! We'll see it all then, see it all as clearly as God sees us, knowing him directly just as he knows us! (1 Corinthians 13:12 MSG).

What Dennis and I are teaching you in this book has the potential to save you a lot of time, effort and therapist fees. Why? Because God knows all about you. It won't take Him months or years to figure you out, because He already sees to the very core of your being. That's why He, and He alone, is able to give you Deep Relief, and give it to you NOW!

Have You Been at the End of Your Rope?

In Romans 7, Paul describes a fierce inner battle to control unsanctified thoughts and actions:

I've tried everything and nothing helps. I'm at the end of my rope. Is there no one who can do anything for me? Isn't that the real question? The answer, thank God, is that Jesus Christ can and does. He acted to set things right in this life of contradictions where I want to serve God with all my heart and mind, but am pulled by the influence of sin to do something totally different (Romans 7:24-25 MSG).

Where does this battle come from in the life of a believer? It comes from the non-conscious part of us. That's why David asked God to search him for hidden time bombs so that he wouldn't really blow it later on:

Search me, O God, and know my heart; Try me, and know my anxious thoughts; And see if there be any hurtful way in me, And lead me in the everlasting way (Psalm 139:23-24 NASB).

The Message translates David's words this way:

Investigate my life, O God, find out everything about me;

Cross-examine and test me, get a clear picture of what I'm about;

See for yourself whether I've done anything wrong—

then guide me on the road to eternal life (Psalm 139:23-24 MSG).

David knew he was incapable of fully knowing himself or changing himself. David admitted that he himself didn't know what was in his own heart! David had to depend on God to reveal his hidden, unconscious faults.

Who can discern his lapses and errors? Clear me from hidden [and unconscious] faults. Keep back Your servant also from presumptuous sins; let them not have dominion over me! Then shall I be blameless, and I shall be innocent and clear of great transgression (Psalm 19:12-13 AMP).

I acknowledged my sin to You, and my iniquity I did not hide. I said, I will confess my transgressions to the Lord [continually unfolding the past till all is told]— then You [instantly] forgave me the guilt and iniquity of my sin (Psalm 32:5 AMP).

When you think of this kind of transparency before God, how does it make you feel? Scared? Hopeful? At peace? The Lord wants you to know that your heart is fully visible to Him—even *before* you are willing see it.

So you may as well be honest with Him. That's the only real path to lasting relief and transformation.

Your Gut Is Your Second Brain

Did you ever get bad news and feel like you had been punched in the gut? Some people even have trouble swallowing—or swallow too often—when the nerves in their esophagus are highly stimulated. Have you ever gotten emotional about something and felt like you had a "lump in your throat"?

During early embryonic development, the neural crest splits into two parts, half of which migrates to the head to form the brain and central nervous system (CNS). The other half migrates to the gut, and lines the intestines, stomach, and esophagus, forming the enteric nervous system (ENS). Your gastrointestinal tract has been called the "second brain," because it contains as many nerve cells as the brain and central nervous system.

The emotional center of the brain, the limbic system, relays emotional information directly to the intestines by way of the left vagus nerve, and the gut transmits emotional information back to the brain through releasing neuropeptides, the molecules of emotion.

This is why your digestive tract is so sensitive to emotions. Have you ever experienced an upset stomach when your emotions were upset?

For example, fear stimulates the vagus nerve to turn up the volume on serotonin circuits in the gut. Serotonin is a molecule of emotion that also helps regulate intestinal activity. When the gut is over-stimulated by serotonin, intestinal spasms, pain or even diarrhea may occur.

Emotions Inform Your Body

Suppose you are alone in a quiet house, and you suddenly hear a loud crash. Immediately you feel startled, and you physically feel the emotion of fear. Your heart beats faster, your muscles tense, the pupils of your eyes dilate, and stress hormone levels increase.

Then your thoughts catch up to the emotion, and you realize that the dog simply knocked over a mop that was leaning against the wall. The fear leaves, and your body returns to its normal state.

Emotions are activated *before* thoughts. Incoming information goes to the brain's relay center, the thalamus, which operates like an air traffic control center.

Signals are sent to both your emotional center and your thought center at the same time. However, your emotion forms before your thinking can catch up with the emotional reaction. Your whole body experiences the emotion before your brain creates a thought, because each additional neural pathway adds a few more milliseconds.

It takes longer for your brain to sort through all the memories and associations and perceptions of a lifetime than it takes for an emotion to be triggered.

It's crucial to realize that your *whole body* receives emotional information. Emotions are like the intercom of the body, the communication system. When an emotion is generated in the brain (even before conscious thought can form), a cascade of neuropeptides, or nerve proteins, are released to send the message to every cell in your body.

Are you beginning to see why it's so important to receive emotional healing?

You Biography Becomes Your Biology

Cell membranes have surface receptors that detect and respond to environmental signals, including emotional communication. When these molecules of emotion fit into cellular receptors on the outside surface of each cell, the information is transmitted to the interior of the cell and begins to change the inside.

This process has been described as a key fitting into a keyhole. Emotional information is literally stored in the cellular memory. You might not have realized it before, but your emotions are stored in your cells.

The surface of each one of your cells has identity receptors. Identity receptors actually contain your entire life story. They tell what your life has been like and who you are now. There is old saying about people who let their emotions show easily, "their heart is written on their sleeve." Actually it would be more accurate to say "your heart is written on your cells."

When your heart, your inner being, changes, your cells change. Who you become is imprinted on your cells.

God created us with the physical capacity to be transformed in the very cells of the body. When you were born again, you became a new creation spiritually, and the "new creation you" was inscribed on every cell. As you spend time in prayer and grow in the grace and the knowledge of God, your cells reflect it. When God's love touches your heart, it transforms you spiritually and physically. Change inside becomes change outside:

Now may the God of peace Himself sanctify you completely; and may your whole spirit, soul, and BODY be preserved blameless at the coming of our Lord Jesus Christ. (1 Thessalonians 5:23).

Throughout your lifetime, whatever you tell your cells through your emotions is actually written in your cells' memory. Amazing as it may seem, through your emotions you can speak either health or disease directly to your cells. Whether you have healthy emotions or toxic emotions, your biography becomes your biology.

This fact points to the big problem with traditional counseling methods: Your emotions are much more powerful than your thoughts! Emotions control both your thinking and your choices—and this isn't something a therapist can just talk you out of.

Joseph LeDoux, author of *The Emotional Brain*, says the aim of psychoanalysis is for the thoughts (cortex) to gain control of the emotions. But he admits this is a difficult and prolonged process.[1] So is it possible the thoughts aren't the best place to start, after all? Is there a way healing and relief can originate with the emotions instead?

Making the Connection

As we have learned, your heart has a door. God uses this door to make a Spirit-to-spirit connection with you. Remember Jesus' words to the believers in Laodicea:

Behold, I stand at the door and knock. If anyone hears My voice and opens the door, I will come in to him and dine with him, and he with Me (Revelation 3:20).

How does this connection work in relation to prayer and forgiveness? When you open the door of your heart in prayer, the love of God can flow to your whole being. If the door of your heart is already open to God, all you have to do to be forgiven is *yield* to His forgiveness.

Let me explain how this all works.

Have you ever heard of something called a feedback loop? One example of a feedback loop is when the pancreas increases the production of insulin after you eat. If blood sugar levels rise, the endocrine system triggers insulin production in the pancreas to coun-

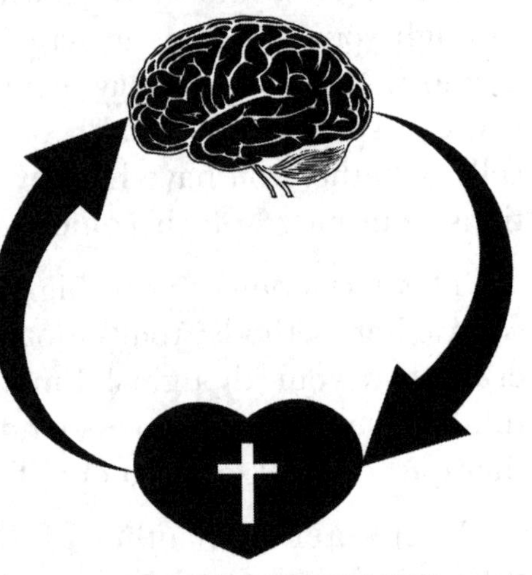

teract the increase and return blood sugar levels to normal. At this point, the pancreas is signaled to stop producing and releasing the insulin. It is a closed unit that operates automatically.

You have a feeling-thought feedback loop that connects your head, heart , organs, and systems. You see, emotions cannot be divided from thoughts. Because the brain automatically links your thoughts and emotions together, it's impossible to separate them. They are inextricably joined as *feeling-thought* units.

The Bible shows this clear interweaving of our heart, our emotions, our thoughts, and our hurtful ways:

*Search me, O God, and know **my heart**; try me and know **my anxious thoughts**; and see if there be any **hurtful way** in me (Psalm 139:23-24 NASB).*

Your brain combines thought and emotion into indivisible units. When an event is stored in the brain's long-term memory, it's saved as a feeling-thought entity, merged within the loop. Your mind and body operate as one system.

This system explains some of what Paul was struggling with in Romans 7. Because the activity in the feedback loop is beyond our control, it keeps on operating the same way despite our attempts to change.

Have you ever said that something "pushes your buttons"? That means your feeling-thought loop has been triggered, bringing a negative emotion to the surface. Every time that button is pushed, you react automatically and negatively.

So does that mean it's *impossible* for change to occur? Not at all. However, it takes something from the *outside* breaking into the loop to change the dynamics within the system. Otherwise, the same cycle just keeps repeating itself.

Getting God in the Loop

The most common approach in traditional therapy has been attempting to force a person's thinking to control their emotions. Counselors and psychotherapists try to bring about transformation by breaking into the feeling-thought feedback loop, also known as the emo-cognition loop.

But this is harder than it sounds. And the counselors admit that if they can't modify what is going on in the loop, the person will be unable to change.

Both Christian and secular counselors attempt to get into the feedback loop and bring internal change in people's thoughts, emotions and choices. However, while almost all approaches try to change the *thoughts* to get to the *emotions*, THIS RARELY WORKS!

Perhaps the following analogy will help illustrate the different approaches to finding transformation and relief from emotional pain…

If I wanted to get inside my house, I *could* drag a ladder around to the kitchen window, climb up the ladder, force the window open, and try to crawl through the window without knocking the ladder over. Or if I decided it was too hard to break in that way, I could just give up and pitch a tent in the yard instead. Sadly, many believers just give up and camp outside of God's best for them.

Certainly, God doesn't want us to give up. But how can we get in the "house"? Wouldn't it be easier to just unlock the front door and step right inside? It would definitely require less time and effort.

In the same way, it's really hard to get into the feeling-thought feedback loop without going through the door. And it becomes "a difficult and prolonged task," as Joseph LeDoux admits.

God has a better way!

You don't need a ladder or a burglar's kit to break into the loop. As we have already seen, God has designed a special door that provides access into the loop.

Most assuredly, I say to you, he who does not enter the sheepfold by the door, but climbs up some other way, the same is a thief and a robber. But he who enters by the door is the shepherd of the sheep (John 10:1-2).

The Bible says this door is in the heart, the seat of our emotions. That's why lasting transformation must begin in the heart, and why it always involves the emotions. The good news is that if you connect with God in prayer, you have let Him in the loop. After that, things that were very hard for you to do by yourself will become easy through the power of God.

Remember: If prayer begins with an open heart, then forgiveness must also start with the heart. And this means forgiveness starts with the emotions, as well as with the thoughts and choices.

As soon as God is in the loop, He can forgive through you. Christ the Forgiver lives in you! Stop "trying" to forgive, and simply yield to Christ the Forgiver in your heart, allowing Him to forgive through you. That is the secret to using your prayer and forgiveness God Tools.

END NOTES

[1] LeDoux, J. (1996). *The Emotional Brain: the mysterious underpinnings of emotional life*. New York, NY: Simon and Schuster. 303.

chapter SIXTEEN
FORGIVE 123

by Dr. Jen

WHEN DOORS BEGAN OPENING for Dennis and me to minister in churches and conferences in 1998, we wanted to develop the best and quickest ways to teach people how to deal with painful emotional issues. Dennis had been using these principles in his own life and ministry for years, but they hadn't yet been known as Deep Relief Now.

I was still new at all this, so I constantly reflected back on the steps Dennis had taken to teach the principles to me. In 1999 we were asked to teach at a school of ministry in West Haven, Connecticut, one night a week for four months. That meant staying in New England from January to the beginning of May.

As soon as we committed to do that, other ministry schools, churches, prayer groups, and even a couple of businesses with Christian owners asked us to train their people. So we worked on training manuals, made sets of some audio teachings, planned out a curriculum, and began to develop instruction methods.

Although the basic DRN approach has a 100% success rate in bringing people Deep Relief (unless they refuse to forgive), some trial and error was needed to develop and hone our terminology and teaching materials. Over the next few years, we saw where improvement was needed, what required clarification, and what should be added. We even wrote a troubleshooting manual for prayer teams so they would know how to get past any temporary obstacles that arose in a prayer session.

This period of time proved to be foundational to the rest of our ministry. Our objective all along was simple: To provide a clear and practical biblical methodology for people to experience Deep Relief from their own pain and then be equipped to help others too. Yes, we wanted to BLESS people with a knowledge of the inner healing and restoration available to them in Christ, but we also wanted to equip them to BE A BLESSING to others through the principles they learned from us (Genesis 12:2).

From the beginning, our passion has been to teach people everything we know, in effect working ourselves out of a job. For our first training classes in New England, we gave people a prayer card "cheat sheet" so they could use it in ministering to their fellow classmates. It was thrilling to see everyone in the room, cards in hand, successfully praying with each other to bring Deep Relief to their deepest wounds.

Simple Enough for a Child

I was once approached by a young mother who was bubbling over with excitement. She rushed up to me at the beginning of class and shared that a bitter divorce had left her and her two young sons very wounded. But she had used the prayer card to lead her sons, age 7 and

10, in forgiving their father. "Right before my eyes," she told me, "I saw a visible change in my sons' countenances as their pain left. They've been amazingly different since I prayed with them. And now the 10-year-old is even helping other children pray through their heart woundings!"

This young mom's story really inspired me. Somehow even back then, we had simplified the process so much that both adults and children could use it in their own healing and in helping others.

When one person or married couple receives Deep Relief, it benefits them personally but there is a ripple effect that extends to the next generation.

This ignited a brand-new dream in my heart. Wouldn't it be wonderful if parents, school teachers, and everyone who ministers to teens and children could impart these principles? I can envision an entire generation of young people in the church who could grow up without the burden of painful emotional baggage. They could grow up to be emotionally healthy spouses who wouldn't destroy their marriages. They could become parents who don't pass along toxic emotions and destructive behavior patterns to the next generation.

First-Feel-Forgive

What you will learn in this chapter came out of a two-session retreat I did for some hurting women in a rustic setting. I was there with two goals in mind: bringing Deep Relief to these women's hearts and providing them with tools they could take with them to help others.

During the evening session, I taught for a while, then offered to minister for as long as anyone still wanted prayer. There were lots of tears, then lots of healing, joy and freedom that night.

For the morning session, I prayed, "Lord, how can I give them something simpler, more effective, and easier to remember than what Dennis and I have used before?" The principles were clearly bringing Deep Relief and transformation, but I wanted to make sure they were packaged in such a simple way that people could continue using them in their daily lives.

Quickly responding to my prayer, the Lord gave me three words: *First, Feel, Forgive.* I immediately realized that these three words were a shorthand version of the steps and sequence of prayer we had been following. And I saw that the body of Christ could be radically healed if believers knew and applied only these three simple steps: First-Feel-Forgive.

First, feel, forgive.

These are the three simple steps to healing: First, feel, forgive. Forgive 1-2-3. If you follow this 1-2-3 process, your longstanding emotional pain can be healed quickly and completely—no person is too damaged, no pain is too great.

You see, the DRN principles aren't just a nice theory. They really work. I've seen countless transformations, beginning with my own story, and in the lives of many, many others.

An Example From My Own Life

I originally had a horrible fear of public speaking. During graduate school, I could hardly even do an oral presentation. Despite having a great desire to teach, I would get so scared that my skin would feel cold and clammy. And as I started to speak, I would freeze up and stumble over my words, forgetting what I wanted to say.

Dennis and I had been married almost a year when he was asked to do a seminar at a local church. Let me be clear: *He* was going to do a seminar, and *I* was going just to *listen* to him teach. Ha! Two days before the seminar, Dennis said I should do half of the teachings.

My mouth dropped open as I exclaimed, "I can't do that, Dennis! I would have to pray and prepare at least 20 hours to be able to stand up in front of a crowd and speak! Since I don't have time to do that, there's no way I can help teach the seminar." Patiently but firmly, he replied, "You know the material really well, and it's not normal to be so afraid to speak when you have so much to share. Sit down and let's pray right now to get to the root of that!"

Dennis then asked me, "Who is the first person or situation that comes to your mind?" As soon as I closed my eyes in prayer, I saw myself as a little girl in first grade. However, my first thought was, "That's so silly. What does that have to do with anything?"

I remembered leaving the school playground at recess and coming into the building to use the restroom. But I got lost in the halls, couldn't find the restroom, and then couldn't find my way back outside to get help from my teacher.

As I described this scene to Dennis, he told me to let myself *feel the emotion* attached to my memories. Much to my surprise, I felt fear in my gut, almost to the point of panic.

Prior to this, I had absolutely no idea any fear from that situation was still residing in my heart. If another person had frightened me, I would have needed to forgive them. But in this case, there was no one to forgive. I had caused the situation all by myself. So Dennis told me to receive forgiveness for allowing that fear to come in. And as soon as I yielded to forgiveness from Christ the Forgiver in me, the fear left and I instantly felt peace.

You may be asking at this point, "What does any of this have to do with your fear of teaching, Dr. Jen?" Well, two days later I taught my half of the seminar without fear, and I haven't stopped teaching since.

Now I *love* teaching! I don't get even the least bit nervous. But how amazing it was that a so-called "little thing," occurring many years ago, had been blocking a major part of God's plan for my life.

Experiences like this helped me learn to quickly deal with whatever issues God brings up. The Lord is *really smart*, and He can see things in my heart that I'm unable to see yet. I saw that all my psychological analysis is of no consequence compared to the wisdom of God.

Try It for Yourself

So how does First-Feel-Forgive work in practice? Here's an outline of how you can try it now for yourself.

As you close your eyes and pray, yield to Christ in your heart. You are opening your heart to Him so He can reveal any areas that need to be sanctified through prayer and forgiveness.

1. **FIRST.** *Focus on the first person or situation that comes to mind.*

   What is the first real person or memory that you think of? Don't dismiss it if it seems insignificant or you don't understand why you thought of it. God knows the order to go in, and sometimes the issues that seem small to us have tremendous significance in our lives. After I experienced that healing from the fear I experienced when getting lost in first grade, I learned to just go with whatever comes to mind.

2. **FEEL.** *Feel the negative emotion that you felt when the situation occurred.*

You only have to feel the negative emotion momentarily, but when you allow the Lord to cleanse the pain, your reward will be a lifetime of peace in that area. Pay attention to how the emotion feels inside you. It has been residing in you ever since the event happened, even if it's been hiding beneath the surface of your conscious thoughts most of the time. Remember: Unresolved emotions are stored in your brain's long-term memory and in the cellular memory of your entire body. However, God can heal these once they are brought to light. As you present your heart to Him for transformation, he not only *reveals*, but He also *heals*.

3. **FORGIVE.** *Let a river of forgiveness flow until the negative emotion changes to peace.*

Yield to Christ the Forgiver who lives within. He is the One who does the forgiving. Forgiveness may be directed either toward God, yourself, or other people. Sometimes you will have to forgive in more than one direction. For example, a person who was molested might be angry at the perpetrator, blame themselves for not stopping it somehow, and feel hurt and disappointed with God because it was allowed to happen. When in doubt, forgive in all three directions, because you can't forgive too much. You'll know your forgiveness is complete when the negative emotion is replaced with a feeling of deep peace inside.

> **PRACTICE:** Before reading any further, I encourage you to take a few minutes to practice what you've just learned about First-Feel-Forgive.

Keys for Healing Prayer

It's important to review the keys we've discussed about simple prayer and forgiveness. Dennis learned these principles during his over 35 years of experience in ministry, but they are much different from anything I was ever taught in my training as a Christian counselor.

As a starting point, you must remember that Jesus never refuses anyone who wants to be saved (Romans 10:13). You just have to invite Him into your heart.

In exactly the same way, Jesus never refuses to heal a heart of pain. All you have to do is expose the pain to Him and allow His forgiveness to wash away any toxic emotions. As you received Him into your heart for salvation, you must live in Him by continually keeping your heart's door open to His loving, healing presence:

> *So then, just as you received Christ Jesus as Lord, continue to live in him (Colossians 2:6 NIV1984).*

As you practice healing prayer in your own life and in helping others, here are important points to remember:

- Christ is the Forgiver, so forgiveness works every time.

- Forgiveness is instantaneous, not a process.

- There is no "big" or "little" problem in God's sight. It's all easy for Him.

- Sequence is important, so always go in God's order as you pray.

- Pray through one thing at a time until you get peace in that area.

The DRN approach ALWAYS WORKS for a person who truly wants help. It is faster than other approaches, because it gets God into the feeling-thought loop more quickly and efficiently. Transformation occurs when God touches the heart and heals negative emotions and inner wounds that may have caused distress for years.

One Last Story!

It is a very dramatic story, and I must say that I have never seen the Lord deal with so many significant traumas all at one time. So I am glad that we had a roomful of witnesses during this particular prayer session. Dennis and I were driving with a group of pastors in Canada, and were in transit somewhere between two different provinces. It was quite a long distance, so we stopped to spend the night halfway, where we had been asked to have dinner and participate in a small house meeting afterward.

After the meeting was underway, a Micmac Indian woman suddenly had an emotional meltdown, wailing, "It's so much. My whole life, I want more of God, but my whole life, it's just too much! You don't understand!" Well, the other pastors in the room immediately called us over. Dennis said to her, "Just calm down, it's okay. We are going to go through just one thing at a time. It is all right. Now, just one at a time. People may not understand, but Jesus understands. What is the first person or situation that you see? Just stay focused on the first one that comes to mind. As soon as you get peace on that one, we'll deal with the next."

Dennis and I then prayed her through five major traumas. Being physically beaten as a child, sexual molestation, having three abortions, rape, and seeing her son murdered right before her eyes on the reservation. We led her through prayer, and she experienced peace each time before going any further. In under twenty minutes, she was not only at peace, she was actually joyful to be experiencing so much freedom.

Then she said, "Teach me how to do this. Explain to me what you did because I have to take this with me. I want to know how to help all those other hurting people on the reservation." So we gave her a mini-class right then and there. She left the meeting later with a glow on her face and a package of How-To training materials in her hand.

There is nothing that can compare to the joy of helping people who are ignited with a passion to bring healing to others.

These champions for the Lord are *Storm Chasers*, because they are equipped and fervent to proclaim the good news of peace to the hearts of wounded souls. They don't run *from* the storms, they run *to* the storms (Isaiah 52:7):

> *How beautiful upon the mountains Are the feet of him who brings good news, Who proclaims peace, Who brings glad tidings of good things, Who proclaims salvation, Who says to Zion, "Your God reigns!"*

So now you have the basic tools you need for receiving Deep Relief Now. Are you ready for a transformed life—and a life that can bring transformation to others as well?

chapter SEVENTEEN
ARE YOU READY TO RECEIVE DEEP RELIEF *NOW?*

by Dennis

- **DO YOU WANT TO BE HEALED?** If you do we have resources available. Surprisingly enough, not everyone does. Jesus addressed this issue in John 5:5-7. He asked the man who had a spirit of infirmity, "Wilt thou be made whole?"

- We encourage you to read the DRN testimonials in the Appendix to build your faith for the kind of transformation the Lord can bring in your own life. Pray for yourself, using the First-Feel-Forgive model. After you experience the power of God working in your own life through these simple steps, show this book to others who need DRN and healing prayer.

- Visit our websites Forgive123.com and DeepReliefNow.com for additional resources and information. We have an online store with books and materials designed to teach the How-To's.

- The Simple Prayer DVD and CD set that functions as a healing prayer personal trainer. In this set Dennis coaches you through the steps, so you pray through the DRN steps with the Healing Prayer CD as your guide.

- This book, *Deep Relief Now*, only covers the basics. If you want to delve deeper, we have instruction on how to deal with thoughts and mental strongholds, generational sin, sexual issues, the impact of prayer on cellular biology and physical healing, and much more.

- Do you feel that you are called to become a minister of DRN and want to train others? We have developed a boot camp of practical training, a course of intensive study, through TEAM Embassy.

- The DRN basic tool is a blue 3 x 5 card called, appropriately enough, the Blue Card, which is small enough to keep in your pocket for reference. Why is it blue? Blue is the color of revelation! It outlines the First-Feel-Forgive steps, with two additional steps that are only needed occasionally. If you mastered only the Blue Card you could become healed and whole in a very short period of time.

- Suppose you had 100 serious traumas, and we have never met anyone who had that much damage. That would seem overwhelming to most people. However, if you used the Blue Card to pray through just one a day, it would only take 3 months and 10 days to pray through them all. And if you prayed through 3 a day, it would just take one month and 3 days. How does that compare to years of traditional counseling?

- What if you then took the Blue Card and taught these steps to others? You could have healed friends and family members (if they want to be healed). Whole church congregations could be healed. Children could learn these simple steps and not grow up with all the baggage that ruins lives, destroys marriages, and wounds their own offspring, passing the damage along to the next generation. We have prototype churches where the pastors testify, "We have a healthy church thanks to DRN!"

The principles of the **Blue Card** are simply a description of the way I observed the Holy Spirit working during prayer sessions. Again, it is not a method, but this is the way the Lord moved to first bring healing in my own life, and then how the Holy Spirit later touched the lives of others over the years. I simply followed the leading of the Holy Spirit. Now I can see God's wisdom in this pattern.

Several years after Jen and I were married, the Lord gave revelation of a shorthand way to help people remember the simple DRN steps. It started with First, Feel, Forgive, and we later added two more steps, Fact and Fill: First-Feel-Forgive-Fact-Fill. (Most of the time you will need only 1-2-3.)

Here are the steps included on the Blue Card:

Make the Blue Card and the DRN steps part of your life and share what you have learned with others!

"We use our powerful God-tools for . . . fitting every loose thought and emotion and impulse into the structure of life shaped by Christ. Our tools are ready at hand for clearing the ground of every obstruction and building lives of obedience into maturity" (2 Corinthians 10:3-6 MSG).

BLUE CARD

PRAYER—Minister under the umbrella of prayer. "Close your eyes and pray."

1. **FIRST**—"What is the first person or situation that comes to mind?"

2. **FEEL**—"Allow yourself to feel the emotion."

3. **FORGIVE**—"Let Christ the Forgiver forgive through you. Allow a river of forgiveness to flow through the negative emotion until it changes to peace." (Forgiveness may go to God, self, or others.)

4. **FACT**—Most emotional wounds do NOT have a lie attached. Occasionally a lie may be believed at the time of an emotional wounding and become a mental stronghold. Let forgiveness flow first until you have peace, then, renounce the lie out loud. Ask the Holy Spirit for the truth (fact) and allow it to be written on your heart.

5. **FILL**—Then, if there was an emotional need which wasn't met, such as love or attention, forgive first, then release (use the God Tool of releasing) demands on people, and receive filling from the Holy Spirit.

appendix:
TRUE STORIES OF LIVES IMPACTED BY DRN

VISIT DEEPRELIEFNOW.COM to watch video testimonies of several of these stories.

'NOW I CAN FEEL GOD'S LOVE FOR ME!'

In one of our meetings, the awesome sense of the presence and peace of God was incredibly strong. Attendees sat still for hours in the Lord's presence. Some slid out of their chairs and stretched out on the floor. Even small children who ordinarily were rambunctious remained still and attentive.

Dennis was sitting on the platform steps, and a woman came and sat down beside him. She told him in frustration, "I can't feel anything at all! All these other people seem to be experiencing God, but I feel nothing."

Dennis led her through some simple How-To's in prayer. She had been angry at God for allowing a particular circumstance to happen in her life, but now she was finally able to let it go.

Suddenly she gasped. Immediately, she could feel a strong sense of God's presence. "Oh, this is wonderful...

amazing!" she exclaimed. "Now I can feel God's love for me! He's telling me how much He loves me and is pouring His love right into my heart!"

Later, she thanked us, testifying that she was no longer suffering with depression or colitis. Best of all, she felt much closer to the Lord.

DEEP RELIEF FOR A DIVORCED PASTOR

A team of ministers traveled to Saltillo, Mexico, for a series of meetings with a few hundred Mexican pastors. When members of the team discovered that a pastor was in need of some private ministry, they asked Dennis if he would miss one of the services to pray with him.

The pastor told Dennis his heartbreaking story. He had married a beautiful woman who pretended to be a Christian. But she had a hidden agenda to sway him away from the Lord. When she discovered he wouldn't renounce his beliefs and his pastoral calling, she divorced him. The whole experience left him devastated—feeling betrayed, wounded and angry with her and with himself. He felt humiliated that he had such little discernment and allowed himself to be tricked in this way.

The man was part of a denomination that refused to allow divorced people to serve as pastors. The divorce was bad enough, but now he was faced with an overwhelming new layer of rejection and confusion. His ministry—and his entire future—seemed in doubt.

One step at a time, Dennis prayed with him until he went from emotional turmoil to a strong sense of inner peace. His hopelessness and despair were quickly replaced by new hope and joy.

A pastor's wife had sat in during Dennis' prayer time with this man. Although she and her husband were in ministry and had grown up in the church, she had never seen anything like this. Dennis had led this troubled man to deep relief through steps that were simple, fast and thorough. Amazed by how well this approach worked, she exclaimed, "Where did you learn to do this?!"

RELIEF FROM POST-TRAUMATIC STRESS DISORDER (PTSD)

An Episcopal priest, had been serving in the Naval reserves and was called up for active duty as a chaplain. Dennis and I had taught the God Tools at his church a few years prior, and he began to use the How-To's in his own life and ministry. He was amazed by the fast and effective results he saw.

But now, as a chaplain, he had to counsel wounded war veterans diagnosed with post-traumatic stress disorder (PTSD). When they came to his office, he used the God Tools and got such good results that the Navy physicians and psychiatrists soon took notice.

A PASTOR'S JOB GETS A LOT EASIER

We spent several days teaching at a church, and the pastor asked if we would pray for some of his parishioners. We scheduled short appointments, used the God Tools, and people were quickly healed and set free as we prayed with them.

The pastor watched from a distance and said and afterward, "This was amazing! It was so fast, and it worked amazingly well." He saw that our approach was much different than the "therapeutic model" used by most counselors: "You didn't sit there listening to them vent and complain. You just prayed through a few things, and they were healed!"

The pastor also noticed that instead of focusing on ourselves, we had taught his parishioners how to use the DRN principles for *themselves*. "I have been doing ministry the hard way! This is the way I am going to do my appointments from now on. You just made my job a lot easier!"

SURPRISED BY GOD'S PRESENCE AND LOVE

A pastor's wife in Massachusetts, was attending one of our training seminars. We taught on how to use the God Tools in prayer.

She thought, "Okay, I'll give this a try." All of a sudden, she felt a powerful sense of the love and presence of God. It surprised her so much that she stopped praying and opened her eyes. "Wow!" she wondered, "What just happened?" She closed her eyes and tried it again, immediately sensing God's presence.

Later, she told us the God Tools changed her prayer life forever. They opened up a whole new dimension in her relationship with God and were tremendously useful for everyday life.

IT'S NO LONGER 'HARD TO RECEIVE'

We traveled to a certain church as members of a ministry team, and after the sermon, we were all asked to minister to the congregation at an altar call.

The microphone was handed to Dennis, and he gave a special invitation for people to come to the altar for prayer: "I want to pray for those of you who feel unspiritual or have been judged by others as 'hard to receive' the things of God." Someone commented under his breath, "You'd never catch *me* asking for that! The results could be pretty embarrassing."

Many responded, and Dennis taught them the How-To's. Every single one of them was powerfully touched by the Lord, some for the first time in their lives. As they encountered the presence of God, inner conflict and frustration suddenly disappeared.

GOD'S LOVE FLOODED HIS HEART

A man on staff at a Massachusetts church had struggled to forgive his father for years of rejection and neglect. He never felt like his father loved him or had been there for him. Although his father had not been physically absent from the home, he had been absent in his heart.

Dennis coached him through the steps of prayer. As soon as he felt the pain and anger leave, his perception changed and new clarity came. "Now I see why he couldn't love me like I wanted him to! My father never got love *himself* when he was growing up!"

Instead of the wretchedness of his own pain, he suddenly felt deep compassion for his father. When he released his father from an internal demand for love, he instantly experienced *God's* love flood into his heart for the first time.

RELIEF FROM HIS FATHER'S CAUSTIC WORDS

A man volunteered to receive prayer ministry in front of a whole conference, on the microphone. He prayed with Dennis through a number of painful situations, then suddenly hit the "big one." He remembered the time his Little League baseball team lost because he had struck out in the final inning.

His father humiliated him, calling him an idiot in front of the whole team. His father told him he would never amount to anything, and those painful words had stuck in Phil's brain ever since. As Dennis led him in a few minutes of prayer, he finally allowed God's love to fill the aching hole inside him. The deep torment was replaced by deep peace. His father's caustic words had lost their power over him and he was free at last!

ASSURANCE OF HER SALVATION

A young woman scheduled an appointment for prayer. But when we began to pray with her, she said her main problem was that she wasn't sure she was actually saved.

She explained that although she regularly answered altar calls for salvation, she was never really sure where she stood with God. As a result, she continually wrestled with tormenting doubts. Over the years, a number of people had tried to help and encourage her, yet the questions in her head could never be silenced.

We asked her to close her eyes and pray, and we taught her how to hear God's voice. At last, she could hear the Lord clearly and receive settled assurance that she was His child.

She wept tears of joy as she finally received a deep sense of God's acceptance. She told us later she was now able to enjoy intimacy with God for the very first time.

'I'VE LEARNED TO WALK IN CONTINUAL PEACE!'

"Due to the ministry of Dennis and Dr. Jen Clark, my life as a Christian has been transformed! I used to experience lots of oppression and torment, and I lived out of my head instead of my heart.

"After participating in Dennis and Dr. Jen's seminars, I've learned a walk in the Spirit, live out of the Spirit, and walk in continual peace and communion with the Lord. While most seminars and conferences are all about head knowledge, the Clarks do the experiential as well, so you learn to apply God's Word to real life."

THE ORIGINAL 'DESPERATE HOUSEWIFE'

A New England housewife joked that she had been the *original* Desperate Housewife…

"Before I met the Clarks, I had so much FEAR! Even though I had been born-again decades before, my overwhelming fear sometimes resulted in panic attacks and out-of-control thoughts and feelings. I expended all my energy each day in planning to stay 'on top of things.'

"I constantly wanted attention, tried to be (and do) whatever pleased other people, was defensive when confronted, and shut myself off from other people and life in general. Mood swings ranged from high to low with angry explosive behavior in between.

"On top of all that, I struggled with feelings of incompetence and a fear of failure. I lived in condemnation and shame.

"Dennis and Dr. Jen taught me how to use the God Tools in my life, and I was able to deal with the baggage of the past. Now I practice the How-To's daily. My story is like Dr. Jen's story, because I have been transformed, too.

"Now I truly sense that God is with me. I feel protected and no longer have to put up walls. I am finally free to enjoy and accept others, and I'm free to be myself in God.

"Because of what I've learned, I know how to OPEN to life and people. Instead of feeling insecure and intimidated, I am more consistently stable and 'rooted.' My internal conflict has been turned into inner PEACE!"

'OUR MARRIAGE WAS TRANSFORMED!'

"We met Dennis and Dr. Jen a few months after being married. We had been having some serious emotional issues and clashes that wouldn't seem to go away. In short, we were desperate. Even though we are deeply in love, we couldn't seem to quit triggering each other's inner wounds.

"After being mentored by Dennis and Jen, we learned how to work through the 'First, Feel, Forgive' exercises. They challenged us to focus on old memories instead of the current troubles we were having with each other. We did what they said, and we started seeing results the very first night.

"Because of emotional healing and growth, we were able to relate to each other and understand each other much better. With the simple tools we received, we were finally able to establish a firm foundation for our marriage. Our relationship has truly been transformed!"

PEACE WHEN STOPPED BY A POLICEMAN

Stina had been to some of our seminars, and she had already learned how to deal with toxic emotions and find relief and peace. One day she was driving behind a truck that drove right through a red light. Stina didn't notice that the light was red and just followed the other vehicle.

A policeman standing on the corner didn't see the truck, but he *did* see Stina. He pulled her over and was yelling at her as he walked toward her car. Stina was so shaken emotionally that her hands were trembling.

In the midst of this stressful situation, the thought came to her, "I've got to remember what Dennis and Dr. Jen taught me: 'Drop down and go to Christ within.'"

Her hands immediately stopped shaking. "Hey, that really worked!" she realized. She then got even bolder, allowing a river of loving forgiveness to flow toward the policeman.

By the time he got to her car window, he wasn't yelling anymore. He paused and said, "Oh, lady, I hate going to court. Just go on now."

The moral of the story is *not* how to get out of a traffic ticket, but that when you yield to Christ, He's able to change you and also the atmosphere around you.

'I FEEL FREER, CLEANER AND MORE EMOTIONALLY WHOLE'

"I carried shame around for my entire life, but I paid it no more attention than to my shadow. I simply didn't realize what it was and how much it was coloring my world.

"After using the Clark's 'How-To Tools,' I feel different without even trying. One of the tangible differences I notice is that I now can look people in the eye—something I didn't realize I had difficulty doing. Overall, I feel much freer, cleaner and more emotionally whole than I ever have before."

'I WAS DELIVERED FROM REJECTION!'

"Through the 'How-To Tools' I learned from Dennis and Dr. Jen, I was completely delivered and healed from a spirit of rejection—something that had plagued me my whole life. Instead of always feeling on the outside of things, I now feel a part of other people's lives. The change is amazing!"

'THE FEAR IS GONE!'

"I was always fearful, *very* fearful. But deciding to try the Clark's approach, I 'dropped down and let it go.' *Whoosh*…the fear was gone! This truly was truly Deep Relief Now. What 10 years of counseling couldn't do, God did through DRN in minutes."

'I WANT TO USE DRN TO HELP OTHERS'

"DRN has permanently changed my life, and I've seen it change other people as well. The principles are universal, able to help people anywhere on the planet. I'm excited about using DRN to help other people find deep and lasting relief and transformation."

'I USED TO LIVE MY LIFE IN FEAR AND REJECTION'

"My life used to be lived in fear and rejection most of the time. But the healing I've received through the Deep

Relief Now approach has enabled me to experience being loved and wanted by God. Now I don't fear people's rejection anymore. I have a deep contentment and satisfaction in knowing I am loved by God."

'I STRUGGLED WITH IMPURE THOUGHTS'

"Although I'm a pastor, I used to struggle with impure thoughts. At times my thoughts would be carried away with things that were embarrassing and shameful. I tried to use God's Word to quiet these thoughts, but it still was a constant battle. This made me feel very ashamed and unworthy of God's love. However, with the help of Dennis and Dr. Jen, my deep emotional wounds were healed within half an hour. How amazing, that within a half hour I was free of the shameful thoughts that had tormented me for years."

'SOMETHING WAS MISSING FROM MY LIFE'

"As a pastor, I told my congregation that God is real. Yet even though I talked about God and read about God, something was missing from my life. I concluded that if I couldn't *feel* God and truly see something happen, the rest of the stuff didn't really mean much to me. I used to go to Christian counselors and sit on the couch and talk about my issues and problems. But often I left even more upset, because I had simply churned up all my pain. The problems just couldn't be fixed. But with the DRN approach of Dennis and Dr. Jen, everything changed. You can feel the transformation, and there's proof in your life."

'DRN REALLY WORKS!'

"The DRN approach really works. There are tangible results. I've seen it work pretty much 100% of the time.

And I think the reason it has results is because it's based on a relationship with the Lord. Also, it facilitates a supernatural transaction, resulting in a truly supernatural exchange. This is such a joy in contrast to trying to do everything in our own intellect. As a pastor, I now have new tools to equip my people to allow the Lord to do the work in them."

'A HIGHER SPIRITUAL LEVEL'

"Dennis Clark mentored me in my relationship with the Lord and helped me return to the mission field at a higher spiritual level than I had known before. I learned how to live from Christ in my heart, not just from my mind. I'm particularly grateful that I've learned how to totally forgive from Christ in my heart. Jesus has fulfilled His promise in John 8:36, and I am now 'free indeed'"

'I WOULD HAVE BEEN A BASKET CASE'

"The Lord used DRN to change my life. It has been an amazing deliverance for me to operate in the principles of God's peace being THE umpire of every situation in my life. I would have been a basket case if I hadn't been taught the 'drop down' principles from Dennis and Dr. Jen. I don't think there's anything more critical in the life of a believer than these principles you've so faithfully taught me."

'THE NIGHTMARES ARE GONE!'

"After I was in a horrible car wreck, I was afraid all the time. I couldn't drive my car without feeling panicky, and I had ongoing nightmares. Yet I was completely healed in just one prayer session. I have no more nightmares, no more dread, and no more problems with driving a car."

"LIVING FROM HIS PEACE WITHIN"

"March 2010 has probably been the best month of my life. My trustees gave me the whole month off to rest and pray...The heavens truly did open for me: the Holy Spirit came down as a dove, and remained (John 1:33). I learned how to carry His gentle presence and peace.

Dennis Clark, pastor of nearby Kingdom Life Church, was my mentor in living from His peace within. Before I met Dennis, I often felt the Holy Spirit come on me, but not remain. Of course I believed He lived in me by faith. "Do you not know that your body is a temple of the Holy Spirit, who is in you?" (1 Cor. 6:19). But Dennis showed me how to stay in touch with the Spirit within. The inner walls that block our experience of the Holy Spirit are simply unforgiveness, doubts, and unconfessed sin...

"Now let Christ in you go to that wall," Dennis said, "and through that wall." Suddenly a rush of love flowed out of me and washed away all traces of hurt and hesitation...It was so liberating that I eagerly did the same with everyone I could think of—including myself. As I released every pain to Christ within, His peace flowed to places that bitter roots had clutched, till the peace that passes understanding filled me. "Now live from that peace," Dennis said. "The Word says 'Let the peace of Christ rule in your hearts' (Colossians 3:15). Whenever anything disrupts your peace, submit it to Christ within. Any feelings of hurt, fear, lust, anger or guilt are toxic emotions which can be cleansed by His blood, if you confess and give them to Him."

—G.F., missionary, Belize, South America

WHAT CHRISTIAN LEADERS ARE SAYING

"Dennis and Dr. Jen have discovered a greatly accelerated way of inner transformation, taking what others pioneered much farther and making the healing process much faster."

—James Goll, Minister, Encounters Network,
Nashville, Tennessee

"I have served the Lord for over three decades, and I can truthfully say this ministry is the one that has touched me the most and given me the tools to help others. Since Dennis and Dr. Jen were with us, I have used their tools on an almost daily basis. People are being changed, delivered, and healed so easily and quickly as they learn what is theirs, and has always been theirs, in Christ. I pray this life-changing message will be catapulted throughout the whole world."

—Pastor Shirley Stevens, pastor, River of Life Worship Center,
Colebrook, New Hampshire

"This powerful ministry has the gifts to minister and equip. It sets people free and empowers them to set others free as well."

—Mickey and Barbara Robinson, minister, Prophetic Destiny
International, Nashville, Tennessee

"I highly recommend Dennis and Dr. Jen for your church or ministry. They activate, release and equip believers to walk in the fullness of the Spirit."

—Aaron Evans, minister, Emerging Daniel Company,
Boxford, Massachusetts

"The ministry of Dennis and Dr. Jen Clark is biblically based and profoundly life-changing."

—Dr. Brian Simmons, pastor, Gateway Christian Fellowship,
West Haven, Connecticut

"This ministry will bring your congregation into the very presence of God, resulting in healing and restoration in the family and the local church. Their teachings bring healing and wholeness, enabling believers to move forward into their prophetic destiny."

—Samuel Rivers, Jr., pastor, Voice of the Lord Church
International, Charleston, South Carolina

"What I find most remarkable about the Clarks' ministry is their passion to equip pastors with the 'How-To's' of teaching their flocks to minister discerning of spirits and deliverance, first to themselves, then to others. The Clarks prepare each believer to get in touch with God within and be quickly delivered from emotional pain. This training is absolutely essential, and I highly recommend it."

—William and Gwen Morford, Ministers, Shalom Ministries,
Seneca, South Carolina

"Dennis and Dr. Jen are two of the best equippers I know in the body of Christ today. Not only is their ministry powerful and life-changing, but they are truly masters at helping others do the same ministry as they do. Every time they have ministered here, they've left us with the tools we need to continue to grow."

—Weston Brooks, pastor, Tolland, Connecticut

"I am very impressed by the Clarks' spiritual sensitivity, their gentle manner, and their clear sense of God's healing purposes for the emotionally wounded. Dennis and Dr. Jen bring biblical wisdom and the healing touch of the Lord for emotional hurts and spiritual maladies. Their altar ministry is gentle and powerful, and their individual prayer appointments can often accomplish a year's worth of therapy in just 30 or 40 minutes of prayer. I've seen major obstacles to growth and spiritual effectiveness cleared out of the way quickly. Your people will not only be blessed, they will change."

—Rick McKinniss, pastor, Wellspring, Kensington, Connecticut

"Dennis and Dr. Jen touch the very lifeblood of the corporate body. I have seen their unique gifting of counsel bring healing and wholeness to the whole nature of our local church."

—Collins Lein, pastor, Living God Fellowship,
Great Barrington, Massachusetts

"This gifted couple flows in the supernatural, bringing healing, deliverance and freedom to the people of God. They also have a powerful anointing to equip people to flow in the gifts of the Spirit through impartation and activation. They are hands-on ministers who teach God's people that they can function in these same gifts and anointings."

—Dr. Jerry Hester, pastor, Dominion Church International,
Greer, South Carolina

"I highly recommend this biblically based ministry, which has brought healing, deliverance and wholeness to many. Your church and your people will be blessed by the sensitive and caring approach of Dennis and Jen to setting God's people free and bring the church to wholeness."

—Dr. Dale Fife, pastor, SonPointe Church, Bradenton, Florida
(formerly from The Potter's House, Farmington, Connecticut)

"The Lord has gifted Dennis and Jen Clark with a unique discernment to help believers be healed of brokenness and wounds that prevent them from fulfilling their destiny in Christ."

—Allen W. Cook, pastor, Grace Ministries International, Brentwood, New Hampshire

"Dennis and Jen's wisdom and discernment have been vital in setting up a new vision for our mission of healing believers and building God's Kingdom. Their gentle spirit and anointed teaching has helped us bring clarity to our healing teams and leadership teams. Their humorous and gentle manner was just the anointing our ministry needed. We have been blessed by them, and we continue daily to see the fruit of their work."

—The Reverend Patrick Sean Finn, rector, Church of Our Saviour, John's Island, South Carolina